D1586570

The New

The New Poverty

Stephen Armstrong

VERSO

London • New York

THE ORWELL FOUNDATION
UNREPORTED BRITAIN
WWW.ORWELLFOUNDATION.COM/UNREPORTEDBRITAIN

Supported by

JRF JOSEPH ROWNTREE FOUNDATION

First published by Verso 2017
© Stephen Armstrong 2017

1 3 5 7 9 10 8 6 4 2

Verso
UK: 6 Meard Street, London W1F 0EG
US: 20 Jay Street, Suite 1010, Brooklyn, NY 11201
versobooks.com

Verso is the imprint of New Left Books

ISBN-13: 978-1-78663-463-4
ISBN-13: 978-1-78663-466-5 (UK EBK)
ISBN-13: 978-1-78663-467-2 (US EBK)

British Library Cataloguing in Publication Data
A catalogue record for this book is available from the British Library

Library of Congress Cataloging-in-Publication Data
Names: Armstrong, Stephen, 1966– author.
Title: The new poverty / Stephen Armstrong.
Description: London ; New York : Verso, 2017.
Identifiers: LCCN 2017023903| ISBN 9781786634634 (hardback) | ISBN
  9781786634672 (US e-book)
Subjects: LCSH: Poverty – Great Britain. | Working poor – Great Britain. |
  Great Britain – Economic conditions – 21st century. | Great Britain – Social
  conditions – 21st century.
Classification: LCC HC260.P6 A76 2017 | DDC 362.50941 – dc23
LC record available at https://lccn.loc.gov/2017023903

Typeset in Fournier MT by Hewer Text Ltd, Edinburgh
Printed and bound by CPI Group (UK) Ltd, Croydon, CR0 YY

For Lyndsey Cameron Armstrong, in memory,
and for Helen Hawkins, in gratitude.

The object of government in peace and war is not the glory of rulers or of races, but of the happiness of the common man.

Sir William Beveridge, *Social Insurance and Allied Services Report*, 1942

Contents

Acknowledgements		xi
Introduction: The Report		1
1	Want	20
2	The Problem of Age	38
3	Health: The Rise of DIY Dentistry	60
4	Idleness	81
5	The New Full Employment	96
6	Squalor	113
7	Unconnected	133
8	Ignorance – Unreported	151
9	Divided Kingdom	166
10	More than Half the Sky	181
11	Courage, Faith and Unity	203
	Afterword	230
	Index	233

Acknowledgements

This book began with articles written for Unreported Britain – a project run by the Orwell Foundation and the Joseph Rowntree Foundation in response to the breaking of the umbilical link between the centre and the regions and the absence of accurate, well-researched reporting from communities across the country. Jean Seaton at the Orwell Foundation and Abigail Scott Paul at the Joseph Rowntree Foundation invited me to take part and provided funding to cover extended periods of research. The Joseph Rowntree Foundation's team of local activists proved the best possible source of stories. Janine Gibson and Harriet Sherwood at the *Guardian* and Jane Bruton and Christopher Hope at the *Daily Telegraph* commissioned the final pieces. Without them the book wouldn't exist.

Maruxa Ruiz del Arbol, my friend and colleague now sadly returned to *El País*, co-researched and co-wrote the first series of articles and helped define the mission. Leo Hollis at Verso had long-term faith and showed extreme patience for which I'm exceptionally grateful. Cat Ledger, my excellent agent, was equally forbearing. Mark Martin and Dan Harding provided expert – and necessary – editing; Jim Carter proofread tirelessly, and Alan Rutter indexed order out of chaos. Thank you all and thank you. Stephanie Le Lievre at the Orwell Foundation sorted so many things out.

I was helped by an enormous number of people across the country – some of them named in the book, some not. Particular thanks go to Malcolm Walker, Ian Cawley, Peter Gowland, Peter Robinson and Maxy Bianco in Hartlepool; Barbara Nettleton, Donna Hall, Rachel Stafford and Mike Ridell in Wigan; Daniel Flynn and his excellent team in Stoke-on-Trent; Jim McCormick, Alan McNiven, Annabelle Armstrong, Sharon McAulay and Emma Richardson in Paisley; David Farrell and Lesley Stewart in Glasgow; the diligent Jeremy Bailey, Mike Hutin and Rachel Howells in Port Talbot; Shona Alexander and John Wildman in Newcastle; Emma Pole, Richard Bellamy and James Grieve in Folkestone; Ian Wilson and Nick O'Donovan in Wakefield; Lauri McCusker, Hazel Gardiner and Dermot Finlay in Fermanagh; Quintin Oliver in Belfast; Anwen Hughes; Anne Birkett from the Farmers' Union of Wales; Hugh Milroy and his daughter Vicky in the Cotswolds; Lesley Smith and Victoria Winckler in Merthyr Tydfil; Rebecca Pawley, Anna Hiley and Wayne Henderson at Inclusion Healthcare; Miriam Holland in Leicester; Emily May in London; Luke Primarolo in Shirebrook; and Bob Wilson and Eileen Gallagher in Liverpool, as well as a number of people who preferred to remain unnamed.

I was also helped by the expertise of Lisa McKenzie, LSE;

Rob Holdsworth and Natalie Cox at the Resolution Foundation; Dr Kingsley Purdam at the University of Manchester; Sam Royston and Faith Dawes at the Children's Society; Liz Chinchen at Unison and Shaun Noble at Unite; Matthew Upton at the Citizens Advice Bureau; Aubrey Sheiham at UCL; Adrian Curtiss at the Trussell Trust; the Institute for Fiscal Studies; the Centre for Research on Socio-Cultural Change; Rachel Orr at Oxfam; Mike Parker at the Webb Memorial Trust; John Bibby and Haidee O'Donnell at Shelter; Dr Martin Moore in the Policy Institute at King's College London; and Cathy Bennett at Fingertips Typing.

Personal thanks go to Helen Hawkins, the best editor a journalist could have; Al Deakin, Simon Wilson, Ed Waller, Undaleeb Qazi, DVN and Sandra Forde; Ken and Jill Coles and their family for immense generosity; Clare Birchall for helping me find my way forward; my family for hanging on during the worst year of our lives; and to Rosa and Tess for making everything brilliant again.

Introduction: The Report

The Plan for Social Security is put forward as part of a general programme of social policy. It is one part only of an attack upon five giant evils: upon the physical Want with which it is directly concerned, upon Disease which often causes that Want and brings many other troubles in its train, upon Ignorance which no democracy can afford among its citizens, upon the Squalor which arises mainly through haphazard distribution of industry and population, and upon the Idleness which destroys wealth and corrupts men.

Sir William Beveridge, *Social Insurance and Allied Services Report*

The 1942 Beveridge Report is the closest thing to a British national holy book. It changed the country fundamentally and many of us, myself included, would not be alive today had the eccentric and patrician Sir William Beveridge not zealously pursued his simple brief – 'to undertake, with special reference to the inter-relation of the schemes, a survey of the existing national schemes of social insurance and allied services, including workmen's compensation, and to make recommendations'.

Initially, Beveridge took on the assignment rather grudgingly. He had an unusual portfolio of jobs and views by the time he started. The son of a Scottish judge in the Indian civil service, he had worked as a lawyer, before joining the anti-poverty charity and social welfare centre Toynbee Hall, in Whitechapel, to study the 'causes and cures of poverty'.

When the Second World War began, he had hoped to play a central part organising the nation's manpower, but was put in charge of an obscure interdepartmental inquiry into the coordination of the social services. He accepted the appointment unhappily but more than rose to the task.

When he presented his *Social Insurance and Allied Services Report*, he intended to tackle the Five Giants of 'want, disease, ignorance, squalor and idleness' with a comprehensive programme of social change. First among these, he said, was want. Giving people enough money to live on, he argued, was the foundation for a good life. Health, education and sanitation could not be improved without it. This sentiment became the bedrock of the welfare state – with most of his recommendations passed into legislation under a series of acts across 1946 and 1947.

Beveridge was, in certain respects, an unlikely social reformer. He got to know Fabian socialists Sydney and Beatrice Webb at Toynbee Hall, who helped shape his thinking on social reform and eugenics. He spent the pre-war years arguing that men who couldn't work should be supported by the state in return for a complete loss of all rights as a citizen, including the franchise and fatherhood. He was also far from a socialist – his political and economic thinking moved back and forth between free market liberalism and a reformist state throughout his life.

The central plank of his argument was, therefore, immensely practical rather than purely ideological. He believed that strong welfare institutions would increase the competitiveness of British industry by taking the burden of healthcare and pension costs away from corporations and individuals and moving it over to the government. This, Beveridge argued, would produce healthier, wealthier, more motivated and more productive workers – who would also serve as a great source of demand for British goods.

And he was right. His report sold more than 70,000 copies to the general public, and when the Labour Party won the 1945 election, Prime Minister Clement Attlee created the welfare state largely as outlined in Beveridge's proposals. The sustained post-war period of economic growth and near full employment that lasted until the late 1970s saw falling poverty, slum clearance and the founding of a free health service and education system, alongside rising real incomes and falling inequality – which, in turn, led to higher tax revenues and a rapidly falling debt to gross domestic product (GDP) ratio. Seebohm Rowntree – the chocolate magnate who studied poverty in York in 1899, 1936 and 1950, and who contributed to Beveridge's research – concluded that, by 1950, the problems of poverty had largely been erased, with unemployment falling from its 1932 peak of 2.7 million to under 300,000.

Seventy-five years after its publication, however, the good work done by the Beveridge Report is in grave danger of being entirely undone. The Five Giant Evils – want, squalor, disease, idleness and ignorance – are creeping back into the mainstream of our daily life. Beveridge was appealing to the nation's economic self-interest when he foresaw that a strong welfare state would make for a strong economy. In case there was any doubt that his argument was sound, the bigger these Five Giants get, the weaker British productivity becomes. In 2015 the UK's productivity gap with other countries stood at its worst since records began.

Since the UK voted to leave the European Union (EU) in June 2016, politicians of all stripes seem to have suddenly realised that the return of these Five Giants has direct electoral consequences. There has been a lot of talk about the 'left behind', 'just managing families' and people 'alienated by the political elite'. Early post-vote research by the UK's longest-standing poverty and social exclusion charity, the Joseph Rowntree Foundation, mapped these new contours of want and connected them directly to the vote to leave.

Founded by Beveridge's key advisor, Seebohm Rowntree, and his father, Joseph, in 1904 – a distant age when people who had amassed great wealth felt a moral responsibility to spend it for the good of the community – the Joseph Rowntree Foundation and its sister charity the Joseph Rowntree Housing Trust have battled to understand and alleviate the effects of low income ever since. The Housing Trust provides care homes and supported housing; the Foundation continues Seebohm's research – looking to understand the levels, causes and outcomes of poverty and social exclusion.

In the immediate aftermath of the EU referendum, the Joseph Rowntree Foundation analysed voting patterns across the UK and found that support for Brexit was strongest in the poorest households (in households with incomes of less than £20,000 per year support for leave was 58 per cent versus households with incomes over £60,000 per year, where support for leave was 35 per cent), in those areas with higher unemployment (support for leave among the unemployed was 59 per cent against 45 per cent for those in full employment) and in areas where a large percentage of the population had few or no qualifications (support for leave was 75 per cent among those who lacked qualifications as opposed to 27 per cent among those who had achieved the highest level of education).

The argument that leaving the EU would damage the economy meant nothing in places like Castle Point in Essex that has seen real median wages fall by 13 per cent since 1997. 'Groups in Britain who have been "left behind" by rapid economic change and feel cut adrift from the mainstream consensus were the most likely to support Brexit', according to Matthew Goodwin and Oliver Heath, authors of the Joseph Rowntree Foundation report:

> These groups face a 'double whammy'. While their lack of qualifications put them at a significant disadvantage in the modern economy, they are also being further marginalised in society by the lack of opportunities faced in their low-skilled communities. This will make it extremely difficult for the left behind to adapt and prosper in future.

The Joseph Rowntree Foundation has always defined poverty as 'when a person's resources (mainly their material resources) are not sufficient to meet their minimum needs (including social participation)'. Over the past few years, however, the charity noticed an increasing number of people whose situation was considerably worse. In May 2016, the Foundation added a new measurement to its bleak scorecard – destitution. This described someone facing two or more of the following in a single month – sleeping rough, having one or no meals a day for two or more days, being unable to heat or light their home for five or more days, going without weather-appropriate clothes or without basic toiletries.

Researchers found that, across 2015, 1,252,000 people – including 312,000 children – faced destitution at some point in the year. That's roughly 2 per cent of the population in the world's fifth-largest economy struggling to eat, keep warm and clean, and find a bed for the night.

In April 2015 I met Graham and Lisa Sopp in Folkestone, and saw what destitution looks like. The previous June, the couple had been living in Maidstone; Graham, in his early fifties, was working as a security guard at a large supermarket and Lisa, who'd just turned forty, was a cleaner in an office building. When a combination of workplace injury and changes to staff at the supermarket lead to Graham's contract not being renewed, Lisa suggested they move to nearby Folkestone, her old home town where a few of her family still lived. Her company, Initial, said they had work for her there and because Graham had served in the Royal Navy – he was on the submarine HMS *Conqueror* during the Falklands War – the Royal British Legion said they could help them with the deposit for a new flat.

So they left most of their stuff in Graham's brother's garage and headed to Folkestone with two suitcases, two carrier bags and a tent which they pitched in a friend's garden to sleep for two nights before the deposit came through and they could move in to the new place. It was a warm summer and the tent made it feel a little like a holiday. On 15 June Graham signed on, and they started planning the next step in their life.

And then the British Legion phoned and said, 'You've made yourself intentionally homeless. We're not going to help you.' Without the necessary money to secure the flat, they went to Folkestone council to discuss housing benefit, where they were told the same thing. Intentionally homeless. You left a good flat. We can't help you.

The benefits were delayed – the couple would be called in to show the same documents over and over again – so they rapidly spent the little savings they had and slept in the tent for four more weeks – initially in the friend's garden, then on the cliffs. There's a beach a little down the coast from Folkestone called the Warren where a small community of homeless men had built a kind of shanty town, but they wanted to stay clear of that. They knew this was temporary. They weren't really homeless, they kept insisting to themselves.

Around this time, Graham's shoulder injury, which he'd assumed was no more than a sprain suffered when hauling heavy bins around the supermarket forecourt, began to deteriorate rapidly. At the same time Lisa's job was in doubt. Initial had been taken over by Interserve and old promises had little value. In the end she decided she needed to care for Graham. He was in constant pain, and some movements provoked cramping. Sometimes, lying still for too long, especially on a wet or windy day, sent his muscle into spasm and he'd shake with the agony of it all.

They started walking the cliff top, discussing – initially casually, finally seriously – how they would commit suicide.

Hearing Graham explain how they'd found the perfect spot and how they'd worked out exactly how many steps it would take to clear the edge of the cliff and fall straight down – is hard. He's clearly been a big man, although he seems to have shrunk – he's slim and moves carefully.

The day before they planned to jump, he explained – four weeks after they'd arrived in Folkestone – a friendly housing officer told them about the Rainbow Centre, a church-run care centre perched above a café on Sandgate Street, which offers washing and drying facilities as well as help with official forms, advice on accommodation and supplies of emergency food every weekday morning. From 2013 to 2014, the number of people using the centre had risen by 27 per cent to some 600 people.

While they were there, Graham's shoulder went into spasm and he started having what appeared to be a seizure. The practice manager, Richard Bellamy, tried to phone for an ambulance but the couple stopped him – they had no money. No benefits, no savings. They couldn't afford the transport back from the hospital.

Richard got them to a National Health Service (NHS) walk-in centre the next day and Graham was diagnosed with adhesive capsulitis – damage to the connective tissue around the shoulder joint. He'd lost around 15 per cent of the muscle in the damaged arm through slow atrophy.

The Rainbow Centre helped them find temporary accommodation at a place called Pavilion Court, built as a hotel in the 1950s but now a first-rung-on-the-ladder hostel/block of flats. They had a single room with shower, kitchen and bed/living area. The walls were black with mould and bare wires hung out of the walls. The man in the flat next to them was an alcoholic – he had a white dog that he'd never take for a walk and would batter and kick every time it made a mess. The man opposite had random callers at all hours of the day and night – they'd bang on his door and demand to be let in. On the other side was Craig – a nice guy, but an alcoholic and a petty thief.

The couple were terrified – although Graham came from a military family he only had one useful arm. They kept their door locked and hid all of Graham's prescription pain medicine for fear of attracting junkies. The day we met, they'd just heard that, after six months in this damp single room, they had a one-bedroom flat in town. Although, just as they were about to move in, Graham found lumps on his neck and groin and was waiting for a biopsy to see if they're malignant. 'It'd be nice to get a bit of a break', he sighed.

The Sopps' story is dramatic and shocking – there's want, illness, unemployment, bad housing and, to a degree, ignorance. The things they didn't know – and the things the people they relied on didn't know – made things so much worse. When the Archbishop of Canterbury, Justin Welby, met the couple at the Rainbow Centre in 2014 – accompanied by a *Daily Telegraph* journalist – the cleric told the reporter: 'there is no system in the world that will stop people having huge problems, but we must have a structure of support for people that meets not merely their financial needs but also their need to be treated as distinct human beings of infinite value'.

That sentiment is an echo of Beveridge, who wrote in his conclusion, 'The plan leaves room and encouragement to all individuals to win for themselves something above the national minimum, to find and to satisfy and to produce the means of satisfying new and higher needs.' And yet, this book will argue, thanks to attitudinal, economic and policy changes over the past three decades, the opposite is happening. Those structures of support that have been in place from the family to the state are now abandoning those most in need.

This has not happened overnight. Charities like the Joseph Rowntree Foundation and the Resolution Foundation, Shelter, Crisis and Women's Aid have all been campaigning on these issues for years. And yet, work from the National Centre for Social Research in 2011, for instance, compared public attitudes to welfare and unemployment between 1983 and 2011 and found that the most recent interviewees hold the harshest views. In 1994, just 15 per cent of the public thought people live in need because of laziness or a lack of willpower; this rose to 23 per cent in 2010. Slightly more than one-third of those surveyed believed that most people on benefits are fiddling and that many people don't really deserve any help.

Over the summer and autumn of 2016, the US FrameWorks Institute – which advises non-governmental institutions (NGOs) on social attitudes – conducted a series of in-depth interviews with members of the British public in London, Liverpool, Manchester, Belfast, Edinburgh and Cardiff. The researchers found that the dominant British ideas about what poverty looks like centred on the idea of basic needs – a subsistence-level existence where food, shelter, clothing, heat and sanitation are unaffordable. This understanding of needs is set against wants – resources that are nice to have, but not necessary for survival. One interviewee told the team, 'It's just having somewhere to stay, and having the basics of water, food, somewhere to wash your clothes and stuff like that – just healthy, hygienic stuff. I think TV's a luxury.' While it was clear that the interviewees believed that society had some responsibility to help people meet basic needs, they also thought the benefits system was flawed. Many felt that benefits were 'often used for wants rather than true needs'.

Attitudes have clearly been affected by the way politicians and the British media have demonised benefit claimants for many years. In Justice Leveson's inquiry into the culture, practices and ethics of the press he criticised inaccurate reporting on disability and welfare benefits, saying 'the inaccuracy appears to be the result of the title's agenda taking precedence or assuming too great a significance over and beyond the facts of the underlying story'.

A survey by Full Fact of stories discussing benefits during the 2015 election campaign found the nouns most frequently used alongside the word benefit were cap, fraud, system, claimant, sanction, scrounger, bill, cut, payment, cheat, tourism and scam. Stories of huge families living on housing and child benefit, or accounts of wily benefit scams, vastly overestimate the scale of both problems on a weekly basis.

The report found that there were only 87,300 families of all kinds with five or more children in receipt of child benefit, out of a total of 7,461,700 families – representing 1 per cent of the total. In other words, concluded Full Fact dryly, 'The prominence of this story in the newspaper articles in our analysis therefore does not appear to reflect the incidence of this type of claimant.'

Over the past five years, meanwhile, more than 85 per cent of benefit fraud allegations made by the public proved to be false – with only 0.7 per cent of benefits expenditure accounted for by fraud, amounting to roughly £1.3 billion per year, while figures from HMRC (Her Majesty's Revenue and Customs) on the tax 'gap' for 2013–14 show a £34 billion shortfall between what's due and what was collected.

Beveridge believed in a society where those at the bottom were helped by those who had more than their basic subsistence needs. He saw tax and National Insurance as the simplest, cheapest routes to this. Seventy-five years on, we're in a society that venerates the wealthy and scorns the lowly, and we are misdirected by the absence of certain stories – comparing the cost to the UK of benefit fraud against tax evasion, for instance. According to figures from the Department of Work and Pensions (DWP), Jobseeker's Allowance fraud – scamming money through the most basic unemployment benefit – accounted for £70 million in the 2015–16 financial year, although with some £20 million underpaid by the DWP the state's coffers are only down £50 million.

That's roughly the same amount that comedian Jimmy Carr, England striker Wayne Rooney, football managers Kenny Dalglish, Arsène Wenger and Roy Hodgson and Status Quo's Rick Parfitt cost the taxpayer when they invested in a real estate-based tax avoidance scheme. The scheme – revealed in December 2016 – gave investors £131 million in tax relief, even though they only invested a total of £79 million.

With pension credits, fraud tops £160 million – neatly matched by the £160 million Sir Philip Green and his family denied the taxpayer after funnelling money from BHS through a series of loopholes and offshore companies.

The figures for housing benefit are more dramatic – £1,000 million lost to fraud with £340 million underpaid, giving a net loss of £660 million. In November 2016, HMRC and the National Audit Office revealed £1.9 billion is owed in taxes by 'wealthy individuals', including £1.1 billion relating to tax avoidance schemes marketed at wealthy investors. You would expect at least a similar level of coverage for such cheats.

And yet to blame the media coverage and political grandstanding alone is too simplistic. Journalists and campaigners engaged in discussing poverty are equally confined to a rigid set of stories, and have tended inadvertently to feed the idea of the deserving poor by illustrating tales of hardship through achingly innocent victims, as with films like *I, Daniel Blake*, which draws on the horrific treatment meted out to sick or disabled people when their fitness to work is assessed by box-ticking forms and computer algorithms.

Those stories are powerful – and an important counter to the demonisation of welfare recipients and the low-paid. But by telling those stories in black-and-white narratives of social justice, we miss the systemic nature of poverty. And so, as poverty rises inexorably, we're unprepared and unwilling to understand what's going on. The great danger we face in failing to tackle poverty isn't just the cost to society. It's the risk to our future.

That there will be greater levels of poverty, that more families and individuals will suffer some deprivation in the future, is all but certain. According to the Economic and Social Research Council's (ESRC) Poverty and Social Exclusion project – which has been run by Bristol University's Stewart Lansley and the Open University's Joanna Mack since 1983 – the number of households unable to heat their home adequately has doubled since 1983, as has the number of children living in a damp house. These numbers dipped in the late 1990s but are climbing again.

The Institute for Fiscal Studies (IFS) predicts absolute child poverty will rise from 15.1 per cent in 2015–16 to 18.3 per cent in 2020–1 as a result of changes to benefits, and that incomes towards the bottom of the national distribution will fail to keep pace with median income, thus increasing relative poverty across the board. Although the national living wage will increase the incomes of some low earners, the IFS projected that it would have very little impact on official measures of poverty or household income inequality in 2020–1.

And in July 2016, shortly after the Joseph Rowntree Foundation announced the rise of destitution – the IFS first discussed what it called the 'new poor'. Two-thirds of the new poor, the IFS explained, live in households where there is someone in work. Officially, in 2014–15, there were 13.5 million people – or 21 per cent of the population – living in poverty in the UK. This is not a huge change from a decade earlier – in 2004–5 there were 12 million people – 21 per cent of the population – in poverty. But the number of families in poverty with at least one adult in work has risen by 2 million, to 7.4 million, or 55 per cent.

The new poor, the IFS argued, are a larger group than these official figures suggest, with previously secure middle-class families living increasingly precarious lives and with people cycling in and out of the official definition of poverty once or twice a year.

According to the Office for National Statistics (ONS), average disposable income in 2015 was still below pre-downturn 2007 levels, while for those aged 22–30 average income was 7 per cent lower than pre-2007. 'It is highly unusual to see no growth in working-age incomes over a seven-year period', the IFS commented. 'And with half of middle-income families renting rather than owning their own home and 30 per cent of middle-income families relying on benefits and tax credits to survive, in key respects, middle-income families with children now closely resemble poor families.'

In the name of a flexible labour market, successive governments over the last three decades have chipped away at regulations, turned a blind eye to shady employment practices and toyed with the benefits system, leaving millions of us in immensely precarious employment, offering little hope of changing our fortune. The rising tide of these precarious jobs, unstable work, rising prices and falling incomes threaten to engulf many more of us, threatening our very security.

As neoliberalism and globalisation teeter on the brink of collapse in the face of populist revolt, we can see that modern free market economics played a part in the changes that raised many of the poor in the developing world out of poverty, roughly halving poverty rates in developing countries between 1980 and 2012 according to the World Bank. This was partly through the gradual outsourcing of factory and service sector jobs from the UK to those countries but also by lowering standards of living in the UK in the name of competition.

The Beveridge Report saw work as the solution to poverty. Since the crash of 2007–8, however, only one in every forty new jobs created has been for a full-time employee, according to the Trades Union Congress (TUC) – a shortfall of 669,000 full-time employees.

ONS figures show 910,000 people – almost 3 per cent of people in employment – were on zero-hours contracts in 2016. These are contracts that guarantee you nothing: no minimum number of hours per week, and thus no reliable salary. They come with no sickness, holiday or parental leave or pay. There are around 1.7 million zero-hours jobs in the UK, as many zero-hours employees need more than one job to earn sufficient money. These jobs are mainly in social care, retail and hospitality. More than two-thirds of zero-hours workers aged over twenty-five have been with the same employer for more than a year, showing that these insecure arrangements have become a permanent feature of working life for thousands of people. The future of work is temporary, short term and low-paid.

Take Daniel Arthur in Sheffield. He's married with two children and works as a delivery driver. Although he is entirely dependent on his firm for his vehicle, and despite the company dictating the hours he can work, he was told he was self-employed and thus responsible for his own tax and National Insurance. The company doesn't pay for fuel or expenses and deducted money for van hire from his payslip. When he started, he was told that the shifts were eleven hours a night for a minimum of five nights a week.

In his first week he worked three shifts. He was told to be on duty in the van and wait for assignments to come in – he only received two or three jobs and he's paid per delivery, so the time he spent waiting was unpaid. Sometimes a job came in at 4.00 am, and even after having been in work since 7.00 pm, he would be assigned the task. His managers tracked him using the GPS and yelled at him to drive faster and get there quicker.

Once he was sent on a job to Newcastle Airport – he only had £40 cash on him and his manager kept phoning and screaming at him to hurry. He was falling asleep at the wheel and burning diesel fast. When he finally got there, he'd all but run out of fuel and had to phone his wife to put money in his account so he could get home. Another time, he was given the wrong address for a parcel delivery – the company phoned the following day and told him to deliver to the new address or he wouldn't get paid. Panicking, he left his kids unsupervised for a few hours. The tension of events like this – leaving the kids, borrowing the money – put great pressure on his marriage.

For all of this, he would earn an average of £40 per shift – he reckons his annual salary is below £10,000, before tax. In the same period the cost of living has risen steadily – households with children have faced an average rise in the cost of living of 2.4 per cent each year over the past decade, according to the ONS.

Margins are extremely tight – one in three middle-class people could not pay an unexpected bill of £500 without resorting to borrowing, according to a YouGov poll published in June 2016. Thirty-one per cent of middle-class voters – so-called ABC1s including professional, junior managerial and administrative workers – and 46 per cent of manual workers and the unemployed would not be able to afford the bill. According to the ESRC's Poverty and Social Exclusion survey, the proportion of households in arrears on at least one of their household bills – rent and mortgage payments, gas, electricity, council tax or debt repayment – has risen from 15 per cent in 1983 to 21 per cent in 2012.

As part of the Unreported Britain project organised by the Orwell Prize and the Joseph Rowntree Foundation, I have spent two years travelling the country to find the untold stories that show how violent the tearing of our safety net has been. I found an unequal and failing healthcare system, housing provision on the brink of collapse, the wilful impoverishment and casual mistreatment of the elderly, a breakdown in understanding and communication between the people and the political centre, surprising levels of digital deprivation, appalling working conditions, heartless benefit sanctions and jobs that offered no chance to build a life, build a home and build a community. I met the Five Giants and they were fit and well.

And if that seems like somebody else's problem – a sorry tale but nothing to do with you – in the course of researching and writing this book I've met many people who reminded me of myself. It took just one or two events to tip them into the vulnerable.

The GMB union ran ONS data on average earnings for 170 occupations between 2007 and 2016. The real value of average earnings for thirty-three of those jobs is down by between 20 per cent and 54 per cent. A further 117 occupations have seen average earnings fall by between 0.1 per cent and 20 per cent. Only nineteen occupations have seen their earnings keep pace with inflation or grow faster.

If you're working in care, leisure or other service occupations, if you're an optician, if you're a financial adviser, if you work at an energy plant or a coal mine, if you work in probation or conservation, if you work in a lab, if you're a paramedic, if you're a psychologist, a bricklayer, a journalist or a police officer, a cleaner or a vet (to name a few), then your salary is heading down.

As Mark Carney, the governor of the Bank of England, said in December 2016: 'many citizens in advanced economies are facing heightened uncertainty, lamenting a loss of control and losing trust in the system. To them, measures of aggregate progress bear little relation to their own experience. Rather than a new golden era, globalisation is associated with low wages, insecure employment, stateless corporations and striking inequalities.'

I am a journalist, not an academic or full-time poverty researcher. My strength – my responsibility – is to meet people and tell their stories. Many of these stories brought me close to tears, but rather than focus incessantly on the bleak struggle they face, I also want this book to be about those people who are thinking creatively and acting courageously to combat the worst excesses of poverty for themselves and their community.

In the first chapter, I'll look at the numbers involved – from the way we measure poverty to the shockingly unfair premium on identical goods that the poor are forced to pay. I'll also look at our attitudes to poverty, because if we continue to shy away from the debate, if we continue to blame people for their situation, then we will fail to understand this new, virulent form of poverty. And if we fail to understand it, we'll fail to defeat it. As these numbers show, that's not something any of us can afford to do.

1

Want

The aim of the Plan for Social Security is to abolish want by ensuring that every citizen willing to serve according to his powers has at all times an income sufficient to meet his responsibilities . . .

It cannot be got without thought and effort. It can be carried through only by a concentrated determination of the British democracy to free itself once for all of the scandal of physical want for which there is no economic or moral justification.

Sir William Beveridge, *Social Insurance and Allied Services Report*

Last year, in Manchester, I met Aziz – a nineteen-year-old boy living in a homeless hostel, having been kicked out of his parent's home after a family row. Aziz had slept rough and sofa-surfed until he found a temporary home in a dormitory at the men's hostel in the centre of the city.

Because he'd moved around for a few weeks, he'd missed letters from the Jobcentre and – as a result – had been sanctioned for three months and was living on a £27 per week hardship loan, a sum that would be taken out of his benefit once it had been restored. The hostel took £10 per week, leaving him with £17 – or £2.40 per day. But he doesn't think he's living in poverty. 'Poverty is kids in Africa.' He shrugs. 'I'm nothing like that.'

There is clearly huge disagreement about the definition and measurement of poverty in the UK – from politicians, academics and the public, when polled. To define subsistence in his report, Beveridge pooled a collection of estimates from his subsistence subcommittee – including Seebohm Rowntree and the economist Professor Arthur Lyon Bowley.

The committee set basic subsistence necessities before housing costs in London at £2 11s 0d per week. Converting this to the present day, the relative price would be approximately £148 using the retail price index. The Bank of England's inflation calculator puts the number closer to £187.54 – or £9,752.08 a year. In comparison a single person over twenty-five on Jobseeker's Allowance is entitled to £73.10 per week – or £3,801.20 per year.

Such calculations are not part of the official measurement of poverty in the UK. Instead, the UK government measures income-based absolute poverty and relative poverty. Absolute poverty as defined by the United Nations means severe deprivation of basic human needs, measured as an income of around $2 per day. Absolute poverty in the UK, conversely, measures income levels against a specific point in the past – most recently, the average earnings of the population in 2010–11, benchmarking the year the Child Poverty Act was passed. It's a way of measuring progress – the poverty threshold is a household earning less than 60 per cent of the 2010–11 median income after taxes and transfers, adjusted for household size and composition.

Relative poverty, on the other hand, uses current income levels, setting the poverty threshold at below 60 per cent of today's median income. Although this definition was accepted by all political parties when proposed by Prime Minister Tony Blair in 1999 – he suggested it as he announced he would halve child poverty within a decade and eradicate it within twenty years – it's starting to fall out of favour.

In March 2010, for instance, then Work and Pension's Secretary Iain Duncan Smith dismissed the measure because 'you get this constant juddering adjustment with poverty figures going up when, for instance, upper incomes rise'. This made the measure eternally fluid and meant that as families were raised above the threshold, the media point itself would rise, meaning they would remain in relative poverty despite earning considerably more.

Over the next five years, Duncan Smith used this critique to redefine the way child poverty is measured – scrapping the legally binding target set in 2010 and replacing it with a duty to report on the number of children in households achieving GCSEs as well as the level of worklessness. In its *Troubled Families* report in 2011, and its *Measuring Child Poverty* report in 2012, the coalition government proposed measuring poverty by behaviour rather than circumstances. *Measuring Child Poverty*, for instance, focussed on drug and alcohol use, family stability and parenting skills instead of income.

The problem with Duncan Smith's critique of relative poverty is something any GCSE maths student could point out – he clearly didn't understand averages. The benchmark for relative poverty is a median measure rather than a mean. If you had one hundred people with one hundred different salaries, the mean average would involve totalling up their combined earnings and dividing by one hundred. The median, on the other hand, would be the mathematical equivalent of standing them in a line in order of income and picking out the person right in the middle of the line. You could easily raise the incomes of everybody below the threshold and, provided they remained below the median salary, they'd have no effect on the level of the median salary. Number fifty in the line is number fifty in the line, even if the forty-nine below them earn very similar wages.

Relative income poverty has critics on the left as well, who argue it fails to take into account the cost of living or the effects of debt. Their preferred measure is something closer to the principles established by the pioneer of poverty research – in the UK and ultimately the world – Seebohm Rowntree. Rowntree conducted three surveys of poverty in York – in 1899, 1936 and 1951 – using a list of essential needs and deciding someone was in poverty if they were unable to heat their home, feed themselves or their family properly and afford sufficient clothing, alongside other basic essential needs, thus measuring poverty by level of deprivation rather than level of income.

This is the method preferred by Stewart Lansley and Joanna Mack, who conducted the ESRC-funded poverty and social exclusion surveys in 1983, 1990, 1999 and 2012. In the case of Rowntree, he produced the list of needs from his own ideas about what was necessary. In 1899 that was fuel and light, rent, food, clothing and household and personal items. In 1936, he allowed that people had the right to live, not merely exist, and added newspapers, books, radios, beer, tobacco, holidays and presents.

Lansley and Mack, instead, conducted a survey of the British public to find a mutually agreed list. In both cases, the list of essentials changed over time. It obviously makes no sense to compare the living standards of 1899, 1936 and 1951 – or even 1983, 1990 and 1999 – with today. Take the telephone – a luxury in the 1950s, commonplace in the 1980s and 1990s, and essential today for those in casual, precarious jobs where being on the end of a phone is a precondition to securing work. Likewise the computer – even in 1999 few people considered having a computer at home to be essential. Since the introduction of Universal Credit, however, daily access to broadband is often mandated by Jobcentres – internet access is an enforced essential for those on low income or receiving benefits.

Interestingly, Lansley and Mack found that even in their most recent work, the British public has always considered a TV to be a luxury – and yet, when asked to imagine what it would take to live day after day, month after month, year after year with just a minimum acceptable standard of living, people are more generous. Since 2008, the Joseph Rowntree Foundation has published annual updates of the Minimum Income Standard (MIS) to reflect households' essential requirements for survival and to allow participation in society.

To arrive at this minimum income each year, the Joseph Rowntree Foundation pulls together twenty-two detailed focus groups with people from a wide range of social backgrounds and asks them what items should be covered by a minimum household budget – including housing and domestic fuel, household goods and services, clothing, personal goods and services, food and drink, and social and cultural participation.

In household goods, for instance, the groups agreed that carpets or tiles for flooring, furniture (including sofas, dining table and chairs, beds, wardrobes and drawers), curtains, cushions, light shades, bedding, hairdryer, kettle, toaster, iron, cooker, fridge, washing machine, microwave, cooking and cleaning equipment, landline phone rental, mobile phones, postage, babysitting and childcare were all needed 'to have the opportunities and choices necessary to participate in society', as the Joseph Rowntree Foundation defines the MIS.

Having drawn up the list, it was checked to see whether it met basic nutritional requirements, then the full list was priced at a variety of stores and suppliers. In 2016, the total for single people was at least £17,100 per year before tax to achieve the MIS, and for couples with two children it was at least £18,900 each – a household income of roughly £38,000.

Beveridge was clear that any measure of subsistence would increase over time: 'determination of what is required for reasonable human subsistence is to some extent a matter of judgment; estimates on this point change with time, and generally, in a progressive community, change upwards'. Beveridge also opposed means testing and believed in certain universal benefits. Instead, from the end of the 1970s successive governments have hacked away at the basic level of benefits – during the 1980s Conservative governments decoupled benefits from economic growth, reduced social housing support and cut unemployment benefit entitlements, and New Labour's policies included the welfare-to-work New Deal and a harsh sanctions regime. Means testing has risen, marking out benefit recipients as separate from the rest of society.

Overall the 2010 coalition cut public spending by 8.3 per cent – over £10 billion of which came from the welfare state. A further £12 billion of welfare cuts loom between 2016 and 2020, including the remaining three years of a freeze in working-age benefits, reductions to allowances in Universal Credit that make it significantly less generous than current benefits, and cuts to child tax credits.

The result, according to the IFS, is that the period from 2015–16 to 2020–1 is set to be the worst on record for income growth in the bottom half of the working-age income distribution, while also seeing the biggest rise in inequality since the 1980s. As a result of these cuts the expected income for an out-of-work single parent is about £214 per week, or around £11,000 per year, and someone working thirty-five hours per week on the national living wage should earn £252 per week, or £13,000 per year. These figures are £6,000 per year and £4,000 per year lower, respectively, than the amount of money most Brits think is the minimum required for an acceptable standard of living. By 2020, the poorest 30 per cent of households will lose on average about 12 per cent of their disposable income compared to 0 per cent on average for the richest 30 per cent.

Recently there have been official and unofficial attempts to shift the blame for poverty to the poor themselves. In November 2012, Duncan Smith sought a new way to define child poverty that was not just based on income. A multi-dimensional measure, the DWP suggested, might include living in a workless household, living in an unstable family environment, having parents without the skills they need to get on or parents in poor health. The DWP backed this with the results of an online poll that said parental drug or alcohol addiction was the number-one measure of whether a child was growing up in poverty.

In this self-reliance school of thought, an enormous responsibility for someone's poverty lies on their own shoulders. And yet the evidence suggests a more complex pattern, including the inarguable conclusion that poverty is systemic, and that while the chances of escaping it are falling away the chances of falling into it are rising.

'I don't think that you can deny that parental behaviour matters and that there are some families, both rich and poor families, who in some cases need to do a better job,' argues Sam Royston, head of policy and public affairs at the Children's Society. 'But that capability problem is not more prevalent in low-income families than in high-income families. The outcomes of it can be worse for low-income families – because when you combine parenting difficulties with a low income, then the outcome's clearly worse. But in many cases families that I see on a low income are the best parents – because they have to be. In a lot of cases they're the best at managing their money simply because they have to. You need to have that support to enable people to bring up their children where they're struggling – whether that's with their parenting or with their income. They need enough to live on. It just seems obvious and it's just not true that if parents managed better as parents they'd manage better on low income.'

The bad parenting doublethink works both to punish and demonise – if the individual is to blame, society doesn't have to take responsibility and can turn away. This narrative is present in much of the British media's coverage of domestic poverty.

In 2013, Christian Albrekt Larsen, a professor at Aalborg University's Centre for Comparative Welfare Studies in Denmark, examined a sample of 1,750 British, 1,750 Danish and 1,750 Swedish newspaper articles between 2004 and 2009, looking at reporting on issues surrounding poverty, low pay and benefits. He found 59 per cent of UK stories depicted the poor in a negative light, as opposed to 38 per cent in Sweden and 45 per cent in Denmark – with child and pensioner poverty stories making up the vast majority of positive stories in the British press. A full 10 per cent of all UK stories had a benefit fraud theme, while the Swedish articles contained only one such story and the Danish equivalent carried none. Stories about single mums abusing benefits made up 19 per cent of the UK articles in the sample against 2 per cent of the Danish stories and 1 per cent of the Swedish stories.

In July 2016, I talked to Sebastian Siemiatkowski, the co-founder and CEO of Sweden's fast-growing financial start-up Klarna – valued at over £2 billion – and asked him about the Swedish attitude to benefits. He thought that a strong welfare state encouraged entrepreneurs like himself. 'If you look at social mobility as the number of people that go from low-income parents into creating a different type of environment for themselves, Sweden ranks among the highest in the world,' he explained. 'I think the rights that we think are basic – such as free healthcare, free education and the idea to try to give each individual the opportunities to do what they want and excel with their life – works very well. Most importantly, the welfare system is so strong that anyone can take a risk and know that – if the worst happens – they will be taken care of. For me, knowing that if Klarna didn't work I wouldn't struggle to feed my family made it easier to start the company. That's how Sweden creates entrepreneurs – and why it's kicking above its weight globally.'

The UK problem, perhaps, is in language. In 2016, the Beatrice Webb Society surveyed the language of poverty and found that certain words caused people to switch off when they heard them used: 'benefits', and even 'poverty' itself. Aziz would have agreed. Instead, the survey found, people in the UK responded far better to framing the issue in terms of fairness. Pointing out that poverty is unfair, the report suggests, is a more effective way of engaging a nation that prides itself on its fair play.

As this book will demonstrate, it's hard to think of a situation that's less fair than poverty – not just because of the huge health implications, the shorter lifespan, the struggle to overcome issues around nutrition and learning support that makes it harder for kids from low incomes to score the best grades at GCSE. Escaping from poverty is getting harder, and yet benefits are still being slashed. Sweeping systemic changes to the structure of the economy have made the only real solution – a good, stable, well-paid job – increasingly out of reach for a growing number. Injustice is ingrained in every tiny moment of life on a low income – simply being poor, for instance, makes life more expensive. Insanely, item for item, the poor pay more.

The American sociologist David Caplovitz first coined the term 'poverty premium' to describe how household fuel, telecoms, insurance, grocery shopping and access to money and credit all cost significantly more on a unit-by-unit basis for poorer households. In 2010, Save the Children estimated poorer households paid an average of £1,300 more for these essentials across the course of a year.

The largest share by far – at £233 per year – is down to fuel tariffs. There's always a discount for direct debit payments, but not paying by direct debit can cost a family without a steady income an extra £71. Direct debits require a bank account, and many low-income families need to feel in control of payments. Keeping daily tabs on how much energy is used via a pre-pay meter feels safer, but such meters typically have the most expensive energy tariffs. Research in 2016 from the personal finance research centre at the University of Bristol found that even a household that has switched to the best pre-payment meter tariff could still expect to incur an estimated premium of £227 compared to the best deals available for those who pay by monthly direct debit.

The next largest share of the poverty premium, at £84 per year, is down to area-based premiums – car insurance, cash machines that charge to withdraw money and difficulties accessing good-value shops. Poorer households tend to take out insurance for specific essential items, like white goods, instead of taking out comprehensive home insurance, but those that do tend to pay a small premium on home contents insurance.

Even food costs more for the poor. Big discount supermarkets tend to be in out-of-town shopping centres – it can be difficult to reach these without a car, and carrying bulk shopping on a bus can be a struggle. Dr Kingsley Purdam, senior lecturer in civic society and policymaking at the University of Manchester, compared the cost of a sample of basic household provisions in the north-west of England when shopping at two supermarket chains and two local stores (see Table 1). The difference between the cheapest supermarket and the most expensive local store was almost £10 for the same basket of goods.

Table 1. The comparative cost of basic household provisions

Provisions	Supermarket 1	Supermarket 2	Local 1	Local 2
Milk	49p	49p	50p	79p
Bread	£1.00	£1.40	£1.50	£1.40
Butter	£1.70	£1.80	£1.99	£1.69
Eggs	£1.00	69p	£1.50	£1.39
Potatoes (per kg)	67p	47p	62p	70p
Cereal	£1.80	£2.00	£2.35	£2.29
Orange juice	80p	79p	£1.39	£1.39
Apples (per kg)	£1.60	£1.50	£1.69	£1.90
Tea (80 tea bags)	£2.30	£2	£2.45	£2.45
Washing-up liquid	£1.50	£1	£1.39	£1.29
Baby milk powder	£9.99	£9.99	£6.99	£11.99
Nappies	£4.50	£6.50	£4.99	£4.99
Total	£26.32	£25.24	£34.30	£34.13

Source: University of Manchester

On top of that come the costs of travelling to work – those on low incomes struggle to pay for a long-term season ticket, meaning travelling the same distance on the same train as a wealthier person can cost more per mile.

Then there's the cost of credit. To a significant degree, the UK economy – as well as those of the USA, Ireland and Spain – has been on a debt-led growth model for many years. As Paul Mason argues in his book, *Postcapitalism*:

The urban landscape of today – outlets providing expensive money, cheap labour and free food – is the visual symbol of what neoliberalism has achieved. Stagnant wages were replaced by borrowing: our lives were financialised. A growing proportion of profit in the economy is now being made not by employing workers, or providing goods and services that they buy with their wages, but by lending to them.

According to data from the ONS, unsecured debt per household rose to £12,887 in the third quarter of 2016, up £1,117 on a year earlier – the highest annual increase since at least 1997. Total unsecured debt rose to £349 billion in the third quarter of 2016 – a record high, and well above the £290 billion peak in 2008 ahead of the financial crisis. Unsecured debt as a share of household income is now 27.4 per cent.

For those on lower incomes, affordable credit is hard to find. People unable to access credit from a bank or credit union are more likely to fall into the hands of high-cost forms of credit, such as payday lenders, doorstep lenders or log book lenders, thus increasing their chances of accumulating problem levels of debt.

Legal doorstep lenders like Mutual, Non-Standard Finance, Shop-A-Check, CLC Finance, Norton Finance and Loans For You send agents into low-income areas offering immediate cash loans – with annual percentage interest rates of between 50 per cent and 1,000 per cent, according to figures from Save the Children. The largest of these – Provident Financial – is a Bradford-based company with four main products: a credit card business called Vanquis Bank, an online instalment loan product called Satsuma, a car finance business and a doorstep lending arm that sends 5,000 agents to collect money every week from some of the UK's poorest households. Its typical APR for a loan less than £1,000 is 1,557.7 per cent.

The company's profits have seen solid growth during the

recession – up from £157.2 million in 2011 to £176.4 million in 2012, £196.1 million in 2013, £234.4 million in 2014 and £292.9 million in 2015. 'For customers in the lower-income deciles, life is one permanent recession. Good years and bad years don't look that much different', Peter Crook, Provident chief executive, told the *Financial Times*.

A few years ago, the biggest problem for lower-income families was payday loan companies like Wonga, which charged an eye-watering 4,214 per cent APR back in 2012. In 2014, the Financial Conduct Authority stepped in to regulate payday lenders and took decisive action, capping rates so that people paid back no more than double their original sum. All the same, in 2016 the Children's Society found that lower-income households have, on occasion, to pay around £445 extra on a loan for £500 as a result of having to go to a higher-cost lender. The Money Advice Service estimated that over 8 million adults, or 16 per cent of the population, have problematic debt, with younger adults, larger families and single parents making up the bulk of these numbers.

Over the last few years, however, the Citizens Advice Bureau has seen another sort of credit dominate those with problem debts – so-called rent-to-own companies like BrightHouse, PerfectHome or Buy-As-You-View (BAYV). These are a supercharged version of the old hire-purchase stores, offering furniture, white goods and electrical items like laptops and TVs.

In February 2016, for instance, BrightHouse – which traces its history back to a 1999 merger between Granada's television rental business and Radio Rentals – was offering a top-of-the-range Samsung 70-inch LED TV for 156 weekly payments of £26, combining to a grand total of £4,056. At

Curry's, the same set was on sale for £1,399. BrightHouse also offered a bottom-of-the-range Samsung 40-inch HD TV for 156 weekly payments of £6.50, with a total payment of £1,014. Argos offers the same set for £419.

PerfectHome offers a 13-inch Apple MacBook Air for £16.45 per week over 104 weeks, for a total cost of £1,710.80. John Lewis offers the same computer for £899. A PerfectHome Lenovo 15.6-inch laptop costs £8.39 over 104 weeks, for a total cost of £872.56. Curry's offers the same computer for £299.99.

BAYV uses a coin-operated meter on the side of customers' televisions – whether the television is from BAYV or not – to ensure customers keep up with payments. If they fall behind, the TV switches off. BAYV charges a grand total of £558.48 for a Beko 7 kg washing machine – available for £249.99 from Currys.

In 2014–15 the average rent-to-own client who contacted the Citizens Advice Bureau for help had an outstanding debt of around £1,300. For comparison, the average debt to a payday loan company before the Financial Service Authority intervened was £530.

'The effect has grown hugely over the last two or three years – it is up maybe 300/400 per cent,' says Matthew Upton. 'The stuff they sell is the stuff people – especially families – need. Computers for school. Washing machines. Sofas. Those stores use all the aggressive debt collection practices of doorstep lenders with the added threat that people's goods are repossessed even though they've paid twice what the goods are worth. We estimate that 20 per cent of rent-to-own customers are paying over one-fifth of their entire income to cover rent-to-own debts.'

Lisa Chalmers from Barnsley had five items from BrightHouse, including her son's computer and the family TV. At the end of October she'd paid over half off on each item. Then her employer cut her hours from 40 to 32.5 per week, and she found she was struggling to make the payments. She sent in paperwork from her company and made an offer to pay a smaller amount. Store staff started calling her, aggressively insisting she stick to the terms of the agreement or she'd lose everything. Over the course of five weeks Vodafone logged over 190 calls to her mobile.

In January 2015, *Private Eye* reported that BrightHouse had paid less than £6 million in corporation tax between 2007 and 2014 on revenues of £1.6 billion and operating profits of £191 million, using tax havens and interest on intra-company loans to hide its money. Our economy has been restructured so that a single mum on low pay or benefits buying household goods on credit can be generating a much higher profit rate for lenders than a well-paid worker with a steady job – and those profits are vanishing offshore, sucking all that money out of the country. It's not only unsustainable for those on low incomes but, as the 2008 subprime crash demonstrated, for all of us.

These are the odds stacked against those on low incomes. And things are getting worse. While there were large increases in inequality and relative poverty in the 1980s, those were during periods of high growth – with at least some growth at the bottom. In 2016 the IFS projection of weak growth, falling incomes for the bottom half and rising inequality is without precedent.

The driving down of conditions and pay has been defended as a necessary trade-off for higher employment.

But the UK has a far higher rate of low pay than countries with similarly high levels of employment – such as New Zealand and Switzerland – and the UK's level of low pay has remained relatively constant for some time, despite oscillating employment and unemployment.

We have certain images of poverty ingrained culturally: the starving African child, the badly behaved benefits cheat. But these are no longer useful because that's not what poverty looks like. People are trapped by cuts, prices, insecure jobs and low pay, and it's getting harder and harder to escape. Falling benefit levels and sanctions not only make it harder for people to escape poverty, the evidence to date suggests that people find badly paid, unstable jobs or drop out of the system entirely. The long-held solution to poverty has been work – but the last few years have seen that principle collapse.

Following the IFS research in July that found two-thirds of those in poverty live in households where there is someone in work, in December 2016 the Joseph Rowntree Foundation reported that over 7 million people in the UK were living in poverty despite being in a household where at least one person worked.

Indeed, as a group wage earners are slowly drifting down towards the poverty line. The share of UK GDP devoted to wages fell from 67.7 per cent in 2007 to 65.8 per cent in 2015, according to figures from AMECO, the annual macroeconomic database of the European Commission's Directorate General for Economic and Financial Affairs. This follows a three-decade-long fall in the share of wages from its peak of 76.2 per cent in 1975. With the top 20 per cent of earners taking 40 per cent of the country's income, and the bottom 20 per cent earning just 8 per cent, the position of the precarious poor is perilous – from 2010 to 2020, according to the Office for Budget Responsibility, prices as a whole will rise by more than a third. Any spurt of inflation caused by the falling pound is likely to raise that estimate considerably.

Since the end of the 1970s we've seen wages fall and, especially for that bottom 20 per cent, job security decrease. Beveridge always intended that remaining in work would be more financially attractive than state assistance, but he was working at the cusp of the post-war period of high wages, mass consumption and income stability, where jobs were interrupted by briefs periods of unemployment. Today's atomised short-term insecure jobs, as later chapters will show, have turned all of that on its head.

2

The Problem of Age

The problem of the nature and extent of the provision to be made for old age is the most important, and in some ways the most difficult, of all the problems of social security.

The plan is based on a diagnosis of want. It takes account of two other facts . . . the age constitution of the population, making it certain that persons past the age that is now regarded as the end of working life will be a much larger proportion of the whole community than at any time in the past. The second fact is the low reproduction rate of the British community today . . . This makes it imperative to give first place in social expenditure to the care of childhood and to the safeguarding of maternity.

Sir William Beveridge, *Social Insurance and Allied Services Report*

In 1942, Beveridge foresaw the problem an ageing population would pose to his plan. He wrote, 'The cost of pensions relatively to the rest of social security will increase inevitably through increase in the proportion of people of pensionable age in the population.'

He went on to make some alarming estimates. Extrapolating from 1931, when one in ten of the population were of pensionable age, he suggested that, by 1961, this figure would have risen to one in six of the population. 'In 1901 there were more than five children under fifteen for every person of pensionable age. In 1961, less than twenty years from now, there will be one child under fifteen for every person of pensionable age, and in 1971 the children will be outnumbered by the possible pensioners,' he fretted.

This didn't quite happen, of course. Instead, there were two baby booms – one following the Second World War and one in the 1960s. Those boom populations are now in their sixties and late forties/early fifties respectively. Figures from the ONS show that people aged over sixty-five made up 17.7 per cent of the population in 2014 – still slightly below the under-fifteens at 18.8 per cent. The ONS estimates equivalence in roughly 2024 – with each group accounting for 19 per cent of the population – before the over sixty-fives climb to 23.3 per cent in 2034, or roughly one in five.

And the Problem of Age isn't quite playing out in the way Beveridge assumed. The baby booms and the unexpected post-war flood of wealth to ordinary people means – briefly – that it's the over-sixty-fives who are forced to support younger generations.

Roger Outtrim is in his seventies. He's retired from the IT industry, ending his career as head of department for a local media group, and now lives in Preston, although we met in a café in Manchester Piccadilly station at rush hour. He's a slim man with neatly combed white hair who spoke quietly in the hubbub of the evening commute. He'd done well in modest terms, he said with a hint of pride – he bought his house, had three kids and he had been looking forward to a leisurely retirement.

'The first house me and my wife bought – we never thought it would happen and when it did, well, words can't describe how we felt,' he recalls. 'I worked overtime a lot and, eventually, we moved to a slightly bigger house. Having a long-term home gave us family stability – that was the main thing.'

His children have struggled to get onto the property ladder – in 2011 his daughter Jess, a nurse, lived in a rented two-bedroom flat with her husband and two kids, and his two sons were sharing a three-bedroom house with a friend and their girlfriends. In 2012, he took out an equity release mortgage – effectively selling his house to a private company so he could use the £96,000 equity the property earned to help his kids buy homes of their own.

The total value of equity release lending reached £2 billion in 2016, according to the industry's Equity Release Council. Research from Legal and General, meanwhile, found money from parents contributed to over 25 per cent of all mortgage deals – with the average contribution worth 37 per cent of an average household's net wealth.

The great reported story in the wealth of generations is that the post-war baby boomers were the luckiest, richest generation – and there's some truth in that. According to the Joseph Rowntree Foundation, the number of pensioners living in poverty fell by 10 per cent between 2003 and 2015 – more than any other age group.

This narrative conceals a number of bitter truths. The first is that about 1.6 million pensioners in the UK are living in poverty, with a further 1.2 million having incomes just above the poverty line. Second, the struggles of their children and grandchildren to avoid poor housing or low income are slowly draining away wealth built up over two or three generations, as frantic grandparents and parents cash in their future to help their children survive today.

Saga – the over-fifties holiday and financial services company – runs an advice hotline for its readers and, on average, 20 per cent of calls come from parents looking to cash in housing money to help their kids. The vast majority of the other calls, however, are from people who haven't set aside enough money for residential care. The average cost of residential care in the UK was £40,000 per year in 2016. In London and the south-east that rose to between £50,000 and £70,000. Saga gets more than 300 calls per week from people who haven't prepared for these costs and have no idea how they're going to pay for their care.

Having remortgaged his house and given the money to his children, Mr Outtrim has no slack left to pay for his own care. He's not sure what he's going to do but he's hoping something will turn up. 'We don't smoke and we don't drink and we've stopped going out to save some money,' he explains. He's worried about the cuts to social care – between 2011 and 2016 local authority spending on care for older and disabled people fell 11 per cent, reducing the number of people receiving help by about a quarter.

Lancashire County Council – his authority – is struggling with some £200 million in budget cuts between 2015–16 and 2017–18. In February 2017, the council warned it would become insolvent in 2018–19 and unable to set a legal budget, with a funding shortfall of £88 million. Mr Outtrim talks about this nervously, hoping that things will change for the better in the next few years in case he falls into Lancashire's stumbling social care system.

Indeed, the entire UK's care system is teetering on the brink of collapse – Age UK figures show 1 million older people have unmet social care needs. The number of care homes in England fell by almost 1,500 between 2010 and 2016, while the total number of beds available fell by almost 20,000. With the number of people aged over sixty-five projected to rise by 40 per cent in the next twenty years, and money to local councils falling, Barnet council produced a 'graph of doom' in 2012 which projected that adult care and children's services will take up all the budgets of every local council over the next two decades.

It doesn't help that the grasping hands of financialisation have their grip about the neck of, among other things, residential care for the elderly. Until the late 1980s, residential care was dominated by local authorities, with more than 90 per cent of beds in local authority homes. For the past twenty-five years this care has been outsourced, reversing the ratio so that 90 per cent of beds are now offered by independent providers. Outsourced residential care tends to be cheaper due to lower wages paid by the private sector. Data from the Labour Force Survey shows that for-profit care homes pay, on average, £2 per hour less per employee than local authority homes.

The crisis of care is fuelled by the slow collapse of the private care home sector – the total number of care homes in England has fallen from more than 18,000 in September 2010 to just over 16,600 in July 2016, according to the Care Quality Commission. The large care home chains regularly brief journalists and complain to the Care Quality Commission that this is the result of not receiving enough money from local authorities for publicly funded beds and having to pay employees the national living wage.

In March 2016, however, a team at the Centre for Research on Socio-Cultural Change (CERSC) – a joint initiative between the University of Manchester and the Open University – ran some numbers on the care home industry and found things were far murkier than that. The problem, the CERSC team found, began when for-profit operators with chains of more than fifty homes grew through the 1990s and 2000s, typically financed or owned by private equity funds. Today, three of the five largest chains are in the hands of private equity firms. These funds use the kind of debt-based financial engineering that suits high-risk/high-return activities, and is completely inappropriate for a low risk/low return sector like adult care.

CERSC examined the Four Seasons chain – owned by Terra Firma since 2012, the private equity firm best known for its spectacular failure when it purchased EMI, alienated the talent and sold the company at a £2.5 billion loss; and for its high-profile boss Guy Hands who moved to Guernsey for tax reasons in 2009. Terra Firma purchased the Four Seasons chain in 2012, borrowing £525 million to do so and, as is the way with private equity firms, transferring that debt to Four Seasons.

As of December 2015, Four Seasons has been restructured into a complex group of more than 185 companies in a variety of jurisdictions including many tax havens – with everything funnelled upwards to Hand's Guernsey base, so that control comes downwards and cash moves upwards. 'It is very hard to see where the money goes,' the team concluded.

'A UK based chain of largely publicly funded care homes apparently needs as many operating subsidiaries as a giant car company selling volume product in 20 European markets. There is no operating rationale for this complex group structure whose primary purpose appears to be tax avoidance.'

Terra Firma's financial engineering adds layers of opacity and complexity, so that what was still (according to Terra Firma accounts) a cash-generative business in 2013 and 2014 became a loss-making care home chain in 2015, when Terra Firma announced it was planning to close nineteen homes in the Four Seasons portfolio. Three charges – a one-off 'exceptional administrative cost' of £99 million, a recurrent charge of £102 million for interest payable on intra-group lending and a third charge for 'ordinary administrative expenses' which amounted to £41 million in 2013 and £46 million in 2014 – helped turn a cash-generating business into one which made a loss of more than £170 million in 2015.

There's something obscene about this level of financial engineering, which effectively takes money from the taxpayer that has been allocated for elderly care and funnels it off via the Cayman Islands to a Guernsey tax haven. This is the money we're paying supposedly to look after those who've worked and fought and struggled to give the next generation a better chance, but it is being secretively redirected into the pockets of the wealthy. Sneaking that cash away with some cunning accounting is a brutal extension of the carnage that private equity causes to any company it sinks its teeth into.

Typically, about 44 per cent of care home residents pay their own way, 36 per cent are council funded, 7 per cent are paid for by the NHS and 13 per cent are supported by their local council, but with some sort of third-party top-up. Four Seasons, however, has about 85 per cent of its residents funded by councils. In February 2017, the big care home chains made a fresh push to earn more from councils, commissioning healthcare consultancy LaingBuisson to produce a report claiming care home residents who pay their own fees were subsidising local authority-funded residents by more than £100 a week.

LaingBuisson's model for estimating these costs is controversial, as it assumes a 12 per cent return on investment for care home owners – a standard private equity rate of return but not one expected by smaller individual care homes. And as the CERSC report points out,

> That is a very peculiar position to take when other businesses like hotels or airlines routinely cross subsidise and never sell adjacent rooms or seats at the one fixed price. Cross subsidy is the logic of the standard marketing practice of yield management through variable rates to increase occupancy and revenue contribution. Corporate customers who bring volume business (as local authorities do) would of course ordinarily expect preferential rates and discounts for block bookings or guaranteed occupancy.

In response to the LaingBuisson report, the Local Government Association (LGA) pointed to central government funding cuts, which took around £940 million from council budgets in 2016–17. Council-funded social care, according to the LGA, faces a funding gap of £2.6 billion by 2020.

As a result of this shortfall, so many hospital beds are occupied by elderly patients who can't be discharged, thanks to the lack of care home places or support elsewhere, that hospitals have been forced to cancel operations – a total of 4,093 urgent procedures were scrapped in England in 2016 for this reason.

Even if those patients can be sent home and receive home support, the level of care they can expect is rapidly deteriorating. Some 873,000 people rely on home visits from care workers, but despite statutory guidance from the National Institute for Health and Care Excellence that agrees to a minimum standard of half an hour, some 20 per cent of councils only commission fifteen-minute visits from outsourced homecare firms. These firms cut costs further, according to a 2016 survey from the trade union Unison, which shows most care companies don't pay care workers for travel time between home visits – which can be up to a fifth of their working day.

'On my run there are a number of fifteen-minute visits – the first is to a man in his mid-nineties who is very frail and slow,' Erika, a care worker in South Yorkshire, explained as she drove me along her route. 'I wake him up, take him to the bathroom, give him a shower, help him get dressed, make his breakfast and give him his medication. Honestly, this takes around thirty to forty-five minutes. What makes things really difficult is the time pressures. I have to clock in when I arrive and clock out when I leave – I have to clock a fifteen-minute visit because it's all I'm paid for. So if I come in and someone is on the floor do I go to help or clock in first? Do you want that to be how your grandma is treated?'

'The greatest shame of my life', she added, 'was one lady with dementia – it takes time to persuade somebody with dementia to let you help them. This lady had terrible diarrhoea and I had too little time to give her help properly . . .' She pauses, looking deeply ashamed and sad. 'And I had to leave her in nappies. She was nearly ninety and I left her there in nappies. There is no dignity left.'

In January 2016, Unison surveyed care workers and found time pressure meant almost a quarter of them – 24 per cent – regularly had too little time for toilet assistance; 32 per cent had missed out on personal hygiene; 49 per cent had struggled to prepare nutritious meals; and fully 85 per cent had skipped on conversation – leaving the elderly lonely, hungry and filthy. A few care workers told Unison similar stories as Erika – leaving pensioners in nappies between visits as they were unable to use the toilet alone. In September 2016, Unison sued the care firm Sevacare on behalf of seventeen homecare workers in the London Borough of Haringey for its use of zero-hours contracts and refusal to pay for travel time, meaning they effectively earned £3.85 an hour.

I spoke to one of the couples on Erika's route – Robert Mistry, who has cancer, and his wife Elizabeth, whose sight is fading. They said it felt like some care workers hardly paid attention to their plight: 'It's like we've gone past our sell-by date, just waiting to die.'

The second half of Beveridge's approach to the generations was the need for more children. 'With its present rate of reproduction, the British race cannot continue; means of reversing the recent course of the birth rate must be found,' he argued. The answer came with the post-war booms, but these were temporary solutions. A report on families from the ONS, in November 2016, showed the average family size was falling. Women born in 1943 had, on average, 2.24 children, while women born in 1970 had, on average, 1.91 children. The replacement fertility rate – the minimum rate at which babies are born to sustain population levels – is two. There are not enough children being born to support our population.

In the face of his era's looming catastrophe, Beveridge suggested the introduction of a child allowance, because a family's income from work wasn't directly linked to the number of children in the family. 'Children's allowances', Beveridge argued, 'can help to restore the birth rate, both by making it possible for parents who desire more children to bring them into the world without damaging the chances of those already born, and as a signal of the national interest in children, setting the tone of public opinion.'

There are many factors involved in the post-war baby boom – including a growing economy, free healthcare, free education and technological change. It is worth pointing out, however, that Beveridge identified a problem – ageing population; introduced a solution – supporting and encouraging parents to have children; and within twenty-five years the problem had disappeared. Since the 1970s successive governments have flipped this thinking on its head, cutting and capping child benefit and child tax credit, politicising childbirth and our social responsibility for childcare and making it harder and harder to raise the next generation.

Large families in particular have been demonised. Although there are large families across all incomes – Jamie Oliver and David Beckham both have five kids; 'mega-mum mega-fund manager' Helena Morrissey, head of personal investing for Legal and General Investment Management, has nine – attacking large families on low incomes, and especially large families on out-of-work benefits, has been a staple in media coverage of welfare stories for years. Research from anti-poverty charity Elizabeth Stories in 2012 found references to large families on benefits more than doubled between 2003 and 2012, accounting for around 7.5 per cent of all articles on the welfare state. Channel 5's factual series *Benefits* offers episodes such as '19 Kids and Counting the Cost' and 'My Benefits Family' and a two-part documentary on one single mum with ten kids.

Since 1983 the British Social Attitudes survey has surveyed the public's view of a variety of benefits – including child benefits, seen as vital in surveys from the mid-1980s to the early twenty-first century. In 2012, however, just one-third of the public thought child benefit was a priority, a reduction of seven percentage points since 2010. This, the report's authors believed, reflected the glut of media stories about benefit payments to large families.

And yet, DWP figures show that 91 per cent of benefit-claiming households have one, two or three children while families with more than five children account for just 1 per cent of out-of-work benefit claims. The families with ten or more children that so outrage the tabloids are, according to figures from the DWP, just 180 claimant households strong. There were 27.1 million households in the UK in 2016, according to the ONS, meaning large out-of-work families make up 0.0007 per cent of the population. The chances of meeting such a household are pretty much the same as the chances of getting struck by lightning – which might make the papers but not the front page, and Channel 5 wouldn't make a series about it.

As this issue has risen up the agenda, the number of large families as a share of all families has fallen. Large families are rare. In 2016, according to ONS UK Families and Households 2016, 45 per cent of families had only one dependent child, 40 per cent had two dependent children and 15 per cent had three or more. This is compared with 1996 figures of 42 per cent for single-child families, 41 per cent for families with two children and 17 per cent for those with three or more.

The cost, in other words, of child benefit and child tax credits are falling naturally. And the total spent supporting all families with children as a share of the overall welfare budget is small. In 2015–16, according to analysis by the IFS, total spend on child tax credit was £21.7 billion, or 10.27 per cent of the total welfare budget, and was claimed by 3.8 million people. Child benefit cost a further £11.2 billion, or 5.33 per cent of the total welfare budget, claimed by 7.1 million. Unemployment benefit of every kind totalled £2.3 billion, or 1.1 per cent – the amount spent on large families on benefits is a tiny fraction of that. By far and away the largest share of the UK's welfare budget is spent on older people. Including state pension and winter fuel allowance this came to £98.2 billion in 2015–16, or 46.43 per cent of welfare spend.

In April 2017 the hysteria prompted by the flurry of exaggerated media assaults allowed a two-child limit on child tax credit and the child element of Universal Credit to pass without protest. Child tax credit – introduced in 2003 alongside Working Tax Credit (WTC) – was designed to smooth the transition from benefits into work and support low-income households. WTCs are paid to those in work – families eligible for WTC receive their full entitlement of roughly £2,000, depending on the number of people in a household and any disabilities, until their annual household income reaches £6,420, after which the amount they receive tapers off with each additional pound they earn. Child tax credit is a sum payable per child, provided household income is below £16,010. Some families are eligible for both.

The basic family element of child tax credit is £545 per year for a family with one child. This rises by £2,780 for each additional child, or £3,140 for a disabled child. A family of four, therefore, was entitled to £11,665 before the two-child cap – cut to £6,105 in April 2017. As HMRC figures show, the truth is that 70 per cent of families receiving tax credits are in work. If tabloids and TV stations wanted to show the truth of large families on child tax credits, they could take Anwen Hughes, a sheep farmer in West Wales, with four children and a flock of 500 Lleyns – a local, hardy breed with distinctive white wool – in Bryn Gido farm, near Llanarth.

Bryn Gido's timber-framed house and its sprawling outbuildings perch on the top of a hill at the end of a bone-shaking muddy track littered with deep pools of water. It's a cold January day when we meet – the wind is so hard it almost blows me off my feet and the rain somehow flies up into my face as we tramp across her fields. I'm wrapping my coat around myself, but she's endlessly cheerful, her tousled blonde hair seemingly rain-proof and her lilting accent giving dreary figures a musical quality. She's of farming stock – her father and his father before have farmed cattle in the area. In 1992, at the age of eleven, she could see that there was no future in milk so she nagged her father for two pet lambs. By the age of eighteen she had around fifty ewes, and by the age of twenty-two she had 120.

In 2007 she and her husband – also of farming stock but a North Wales boy – decided to buy some land. They bought some brokers (old ewes), bred them and then sold the brokers and their lambs to buy pedigree Lleyns breeding lambs. Things ticked over until 2013, when a late spring meant no grass, so they were feeding the lambs all the way into June. Instead of their usual five to ten tonnes of feed, they had to buy fifteen to twenty tonnes at about £240 per tonne, 'so I think we were about £10,000 into feed and then fertiliser went up and then lamb prices went down as Russia stopped importing and the exchange rate worked against us'.

They ended up selling the majority of their lambs through the light market – where underweight lambs are sold on for somebody else to fatten up. All told, they made a loss of £10 per head. In 2014 they got hit with a worm resistant to deworming drench – they only sold 250 lambs through the abattoir and about 500 through the light market. In 2016, New Zealand dumped a load of lamb on to the market, driving prices down sharply: 'supermarkets squeeze every last penny out of you, just so that they can make a profit – you're just a commodity', she explains. 'If they can fill their order with cheap New Zealand lamb, they don't come to you. Some farmers were losing between £10 and £20 per head – we were lucky . . . we only lost £8 per head.'

Anwen survives on her EU subsidy, the single-farm payment, which oscillates between £6,000 and £9,000 per year, and the child benefit and child tax credits for her four children that come to roughly £600 per month.

Two years ago there was a mistake made when she reapplied over the phone – the wrong numbers got put into the wrong boxes and they stopped her payments for six months.

Things got very tough – she was cutting back on clothes and school trips for the kids, cancelling additional lessons and tightening up on everything. Her eldest son has just left education so the credits are drawing down, but if they'd cut her tax credits in half ten years ago? 'No way would we have been able to manage without it.'

'Essentially, under these changes, you're better off if your family breaks down.' Sam Royston, from the Children's Society, shakes his head. 'If you're a couple with four children you're worse off by about £5,000 a year. If you split into two single-parent families with two children each you would get the full entitlement for all four children. It just seems bizarre that the government should be incentivising those kind of choices. That's not about creating better parenting. That's about how cutting income actually makes parenting much, much harder. One of the big issues that the government have talked about is the importance of creating strong, stable families – and they've created exactly the kind of conditions which lead to the opposite.'

Alongside the child tax credit cap, the Children's Society is seeing parents moving one or two children out of the family home to live with a relative thanks to the recent lowering of George Osborne's benefit cap. First introduced at £26,000 per year per household in 2013, and pushed further down in November 2016 to £23,000 in London and £20,000 in the rest of the country, the cap was announced in 2010 under the slogan: 'Nobody on benefits should be allowed to earn more than the average wage.'

Even Iain Duncan Smith objected to that particular piece of political mendacity. At the time, median pay in the UK was £26,000 a year (£27,600 in 2016), but this figure is the gross pre-tax income for an individual, as opposed to the disposable income of a whole family. The result has been to punish children born into large families – especially those in households paying high rents. Research on the effects of the new cap by the Chartered Institute of Housing found 116,000 families, with a total of 319,000 children, lost around £100 per week. A couple with three children now have £50.80 a week for housing costs – while rent for a three-bedroom property in, for example, Leeds is £151.50 a week. One London-based mother Royston's team are helping had her benefit capped at £500 per week so she couldn't afford to pay the rent and buy food for her two daughters. She had to move in with her mother.

Couple this penalising of large families and wilful breaking up of homes with planned restrictions aiming to cut net immigration to the 'tens of thousands', and it's worryingly unclear how Britain's working, taxpaying population will be able to support its elderly population. It's one thing to battle a demographic time bomb – as Beveridge so successfully did. It's quite another to actively induce it.

For all low-income families, there's only more pain on the way. In 2014, the IFS projected that tax and benefit changes made since 2010 will see the number of children in relative poverty rise from 2.3 to 3.6 million by 2020. Growing up in poverty has both immediate and long-term effects – children in poverty suffer worse physical and mental health, while Department of Education figures show a 28 per cent gap between children receiving free school meals and their wealthier peers in terms of the number achieving at least five A*–C GCSE grades. The chances of escaping poverty are systematically reduced for children growing up in poverty.

The last thirty years have played a cruel trick on families. The post-war generation managed to raise themselves up through a combination of hope, luck, ambition and a popular demand for social progress. This generation hasn't even got hope.

In 2012 I went to Wigan to find the children of the people George Orwell met when he wrote *Road to Wigan Pier* – the three whose names we know, thanks to Bernard Crick's *George Orwell: A Life*. First there was Gerry Kennan, the local trade union leader who found him accommodation in Scholes, the industrial district, and took him on a visit to the local pit. Then there was a paperboy – Sid Smith – who met 'this tall gangly man wearing Oxford bags who had a tousled appearance and carried a clipboard'. Orwell's questions convinced Sid that he was a dole snoop, so the boys fled. Finally there was Jim Hammond, an unemployed, blacklisted, Communist coalminer whose wife was pregnant when Orwell looked around their two-up-two-down house.

Gerry Kennan's son worked as an electrician in the pits until they closed, then worked at the Heinz factory, where he fought for and won trade union recognition and made the Wigan factory one of Heinz's safest. He married, had two daughters, and lived on the Beech Hill estate with a view across the town until he died, in October 2011.

Sid Smith turned his paper round into a kiosk in the town's central arcade that grew into a shop and gradually took over one whole side of the arcade. His son Trevor helped him build the store into the largest independent retailer in the northwest – adding books and music to the papers and magazines. Trevor sold up in 2006, just as Amazon ate up the book trade, and lives just outside Wigan in a leafy village. The shop closed in 2009.

Jim Hammond's son Tony was born in Park Hospital, Davyhulme – the hospital where Nye Bevan founded the NHS. He received free school meals, won a scholarship to Wigan grammar school and went on to study law at Oxford. Jim Hammond dug coal with a pick axe, was paid by the basket and was blacklisted for being a troublemaker. When I met Tony Hammond at his sports club in Manchester, he was a retired judge.

The following day, I went back to the Scholes Precinct, where half the shops had closed thanks to the Post Office moving into the centre of town. There I met a twelve-year-old kid whose dad drank himself to death and whose mum was going the same way. He's on free school meals – his mum gets £108 per week and puts £35 on the gas and £35 on the electric. Some days, when there's no food, he lives on a bowl of cereal. If he's at school he gets a hot lunch – at the weekends, almost never.

I asked him what he wanted to do with his life and he said he wanted to be a vet – some men on his estate breed and sell dogs and he loves animals. I told him about Tony Hammond – born two streets from where we were standing, now a retired judge – and he laughed. 'For me to become a vet,' he said, 'you'd have to have some magician come along and cast a spell.'

In other words, the social mobility that lifted one kid from Scholes into the judiciary is now all but impossible – and seen as such – by a kid from the same postcode today. 'If you ask children on low incomes what their aspirations are for the future, they have lower ambitions and are less optimistic than wealthier kids,' says Royston. 'Poverty and debt reduce people's hope and there's a real decline in the sense of aspiration for children in those families.'

The social mobility that propelled the hardworking Tony Hammond into his judge's wig is what happened when a Hammond got a fair chance. In a fair society an individual's chance of building a good life for themselves should be the same regardless of their background or where they grew up. The more social mobility there is, the less someone's destination in life depends on where they start out. Over recent years, however, the link between demography and destiny is actually getting stronger in the UK. Today only one in eight children from low-income backgrounds goes on to become a high earner as an adult.

The 1970 British Cohort Study (BCS70) analysed men over a period of sixteen years, from age twenty-six to forty-two, comparing the income quintile they were born into with the earnings quintile they reached as adults. Quintiles divide the population into five equal groups – in this case the bottom quintile is the 20 per cent of households with the lowest income and the top quintile is the 20 per cent with the highest income.

In a perfectly socially mobile society, the individuals born in each quintile would end up evenly distributed across the five quintiles as adults. Those born into the bottom 20 per cent should spread so that 4 per cent were in the bottom quintile, 4 per cent in the second, and so on. In fact, more of the bottom quintile stayed in the bottom 20 per cent for earnings (6.33 per cent rather than 4 per cent), and fewer reach the top (2.27 per cent). The second quintile – with a household income of around £22,500 a year – found it almost as hard to get to the top, and even middle-income children struggled to get into the top 20 per cent. Those born into the most affluent families had a very strong chance of staying there, and very little likelihood of falling. Comparable data from the Labour Force Survey in 2015 – looking at earnings for those aged twenty-nine to thirty-six – showed effectively the same spread

The remarkable dream of the UK in the twentieth century was that each generation could and would be better off than their parents. This is no longer the case. Institute of Fiscal Studies analysis of data from the Family Expenditure Survey and Family Resources Survey across various years compared average household income for people when they reached fifty. Those born in the 1950s had a salary more than 20 per cent higher than the average income for the 1940s cohort – an increase equivalent to around £5,000 a year for a couple without children. Average income for the 1940s cohort was over 20 per cent higher than average income for the 1930s cohort at the same age.

And yet for people born in the 1960s, 1970s and early 1980s – known as Generation X – this is no longer true. By their early thirties, those born in the early 1980s had average net household wealth of £27,000 per adult – including housing, financial and private pension wealth. This is about half of the average wealth holdings of the 1970s cohort at around the same age – £53,000.

For millennials – those born between 1981 and 2000 – things are complicated. Using data from the ONS quarterly Labour Force Survey, the Resolution Foundation found a split between the fortunes of men and women. In terms of real median weekly pay, young women have fared no better or worse than the previous generation. Millennial men, however, have earned less than Generation X men in each year of their twenties, adding up to a total pay deficit of £12,500 by the time they reach thirty.

This is partly due to the collapse in manufacturing jobs. From 1993 to 2015–16 there has been a 40 per cent drop in the number of men aged twenty-two to thirty-five working in manufacturing. The number of young men working in retail has almost doubled, from 85,000 to 165,000, over the same period; the number working in bars and restaurants has trebled, from 45,000 to 130,000; and the number of men working part-time has increased by 400 per cent.

It's these conditions that are making it hard for younger generations to have the security to settle, find stable communities, buy some property and raise their own family. The Problem of Age that Beveridge outlined was neatly solved. Solving the current Problem of Age while Britain is in the midst, according to IFS figures, of the weakest growth in living standards in at least sixty years, is messy at best. Weak earnings growth and changes to taxes and benefits means income for the average family will flatline between 2016 and 2018, according to those figures, while 400,000 pensioners and over 1 million more children are likely to fall into poverty by 2021.

Right now the only hope for those families that can afford it, like the Outtrims, is to fleece themselves to give their kids a better chance. But this money is finite. What happens when it all runs out?

3

Health: The Rise of DIY Dentistry

Restoration of a sick person to health is a duty of the State and the sick person, prior to any other consideration . . .

A comprehensive national health service will ensure that for every citizen there is available whatever medical treatment he requires, in whatever form he requires it, domiciliary or institutional, general, specialist or consultant, and will ensure also the provision of dental, ophthalmic and surgical appliances, nursing and midwifery and rehabilitation after accidents.

Sir William Beveridge, *Social Insurance
and Allied Services Report*

It was in Paisley, Scotland's largest and poorest town, that I first came across DIY dentistry. I met Alex Hythe, a thirty-eight-year-old building engineer from Glasgow, a big man with quick, nervous hands and an uneasy smile. His partner Tilly gave up her teaching job when their eldest son was diagnosed with Asperger syndrome five years ago. When the recession hit in 2008, Alex found work hard to come by.

He took a couple of short-term contracts, but he'd not worked for a year when he missed a dental appointment – a Jobcentre interview came up suddenly and he'd have been sanctioned if he failed to attend. When he called to rebook, his dentist levelled a £25 charge for cancelling his appointment with too little notice.

'We were stuck in this little flat and I couldn't justify going and getting my teeth fixed when we can't afford nappies,' Alex explained. Instead a friend suggested he buy an emergency DIY dental first aid kit from a local pound store – sold as a temporary remedy for lost fillings, caps and crowns – and start treating his own teeth.

Alex bought a Poundland own-brand Dental Tool Kit – which includes a small mirror, a scaler and a dental pick and is marketed as a safe way to locate and remove 'stains, plaque, bacterial debris and food debris from both sides of and between teeth' – as well as a DenTek Dental First Aid Kit, which comes with a small phial of eugenol, which has anaesthetic and antibacterial properties, a phial of Temparin Max, a soft material that sets in the mouth to repair lost fillings, caps or crowns, and a tiny spatula. All in, he paid less than £10.

With Tilly's help, Alex crouched in the bathroom and started scraping away at his damaged filling. The first pass proved too painful even with the eugenol – he dropped the pick and couldn't find it for the tears in his eyes – so he took four Paracetamol and tried again. Eventually, he'd pulled out what he considered to be a filling-sized amount of material from the bad tooth and stuffed the Temparin in as best he could, trying to use the dentist mirror and the bathroom mirror to check it looked OK. He couldn't bite down comfortably, but the pain had diminished.

'DIY dentistry is fairly common round here,' explained Emma Richardson, project development coordinator at the Star Project in Paisley, Renfrewshire, just along the road from Alan's flat. On an afternoon in the Star Project I met people who'd bought DIY kits online, from pound shops or even from friends to do their own fillings, and people who passed around unfinished courses of sedatives, antidepressants, beta blockers and even antibiotics. The community almost seemed to run its own shadow health service. 'DIY is just cheaper than the dentist,' said one young mother. 'My uncle takes care of his teeth and everyone in his family.'

Alice – one of the Star Project's service users – resorted to popping her own mouth abscess with a fork since she was worried about a fine for a missed appointment and the costs of treatment. Her partner had been sanctioned for arriving late at a Jobcentre interview, leaving the couple with around £65 per week, out of which they paid £10 for gas and £10 for electricity – 'I have to sign on every week which is a £3.60 bus ticket,' Alice explains. 'When you add in TV licence and phone calls you've got £25 per week, which has to cover food for a family of four.'

The NHS, of course, was designed to provide healthcare that was comprehensive, universal and free at the point of delivery. Beveridge had identified a national health service as one of three essential elements of a viable social security system – the other two being child benefit and full employment. Before the NHS, there was a rudimentary National Health Insurance scheme for low-income working men but not their families. It bestowed limited GP (general practitioner) care and covered hospital admission only in the case of tuberculosis. Voluntary hospitals were supported by donations but frequently ran out of money – the 1930s were particularly hard.

People who had no formal health cover had to use self-medication or over-the-counter drugs from a chemist. An illness, or paying for a doctor or midwife to be present at a birth, could cause major financial problems for families across the country. The NHS changed this, using GPs and dentists operating in the community as the front line of the service, dealing with or referring patients. Prescriptions rose from 5 million a month before the NHS to 13.5 million in September 1948 – in the first year 8 million dental patients were treated.

Over the past twenty years, however, changes to every-thing from the way dentists are paid to the move to phone and online bookings for GP appointments mean the system is no longer able to honour that promise. The truth is that poverty, inequality and the increasing stigma attached to both are blocking access to healthcare for the poorest people in the UK.

In fact, Alice and Alex were luckier than most Brits in their access to free dentistry – dental examinations are free in Scotland and Northern Ireland, with the patient only incurring the cost of treatment. It's technically not allowed for dentists to levy fines in the way that scared Alex, but many do.

Accurate figures on the extent of DIY dentistry are hard to find. One of the biggest sellers of dental first aid kits, DenTek, shifts over 250,000 kits a year, but there's no research on how people use the kit. In researching this book I met people in Hartlepool, Merthyr Tydfil and Bristol who had worked on their own mouths with these kits. In 2012, research from the oral health charity the British Dental Health Foundation found that one in five Britons would remove a tooth themselves or ask a friend to do so if they couldn't afford dental treatment. The Foundation hasn't followed this up, explains its dental advisor Karen Coates, because 'all of the stuff that we have is anecdotal'.

And yet any and all figures on DIY dentistry and the black health economy will necessarily be anecdotal, according to John Wildman, professor of health economics at Newcastle University. The way we gather health data relies on surveys and GP-based patient interaction. 'People at the lower end of the distribution curve – on big housing estates in the north-east, for instance – are effectively completely unreported,' he explained. 'They don't take part in surveys and they don't go in to GP surgeries. Which is why you have a situation where people in the north-east have gaps in their teeth and are resorting to DIY dentistry while at the other end of the scale there are people for whom toothpaste isn't even about fighting infection – it's about making their teeth whiter. It's crazy.'

This is an almost Victorian idea of hardship that is shocking in a country that prides itself on free healthcare. Paisley's long, slow decline itself is bleak testament to the chaotic deindustrialisation of the late 1970s and 1980s. The town was built on the weaving trade, then rode the boom in shipbuilding and construction along the Clyde. Just before the Second World War, Paisley boasted five shipyards with associated engineering companies, the Linwood car factory, whisky producer William Grant and Sons, Robertson's jam and marmalades and two huge mills – Anchor and Ferguslie

– which between them employed 30,000 people and produced the famous Paisley pattern, based on an ancient Persian design. By the end of the 1980s, however, all of these had closed or moved out of the town.

Since then, Paisley has struggled. In 2012, according to figures from the Local Data Company, the town had the greatest number of store vacancies in Scotland with almost 30 per cent of shops shuttered. When I visited the town in 2015 and 2016, roughly half the shops in the high street stood empty. Marks and Spencer and WHSmith were among the few chains that remained.

The Ferguslie Park estate – a hastily thrown together piece of 1930s slum clearance that used to surround the Ferguslie mills and Linwood's car plant – was named the poorest area in Scotland in 2006, 2012 and, most recently, in August 2016. The estate is difficult to reach, cut off from Glasgow Airport by a road and railway line. Much of the housing stock is new and there's a modern community centre, although there are streets lined with boarded-up houses and gardens littered with abandoned furniture. No one passes through. The whole estate feels isolated and ignored.

And yet Paisley is far from isolated in dealing with the collapse of acceptable healthcare for low-income families. Oral health inequality is particularly bad, according to Jack Toumba, professor of paediatric dentistry at the University of Leeds faculty of medicine and health, because dentistry has effectively been privatised. Although there are practices offering NHS care, Toumba's concern is that they are increasingly hard to find.

'We're finding patients who've rung practices across the north asking to register as an NHS patient only to be told the

NHS lists are full and they can only register as a private patient,' he explains. He cites one patient – a forty-year-old HGV driver – who used the plastic mirror, forceps and probe from an over-the-counter dental kit to clean and prepare a cavity before plugging the hole with Quick Steel, a potentially toxic steel-reinforced epoxy putty used to fix engines. 'His local dentist had discontinued NHS dental services and he couldn't afford private dental care or find another NHS dentist. He'd treated the tooth twice by himself in the three years before he came to see us.'

This has prompted DentAid – a Salisbury-based dental NGO set up in 1996 to improve oral health in the developing world – to launch its first UK-based projects. The charity – which offers portable dental surgeries to struggling communities in Uganda, Malawi, Cambodia and Romania – started funding emergency dentists' clinics and a mobile van in the UK in 2015.

One of their first projects was the Real Junk Tooth Project in Dewsbury. The West Yorkshire town was once famous for manufacturing wool products: the town claimed it provided the coats for British soldiers' backs and the blankets under which they slept. As the mills left, deprivation increased, and families shipped over from India and Pakistan to work in the mills were hardest hit. Today, 20 per cent of working-age adults live in poverty – as do 27 per cent of children and 45 per cent of pensioners. Thirty-three per cent of working adults in Dewsbury are unemployed, and one in four are in routine and manual work.

In 2015, Dewsbury dentist Nick O'Donovan visited a local food charity, the Real Junk Food Project, which uses food donations from supermarkets to make healthy meals and charges people what they think the meal is worth. If customers have no money, they can volunteer labour and skills instead. O'Donovan found that many people who used the project were struggling to chew the food they were being given as their teeth were decaying or in pain.

With help from DentAid, O'Donovan set up a weekly free clinic advertising through the Real Junk Food café. It operated on the 'pay if you can' principle and ran from December 2015 until June 2016. 'The mouths that we saw looked like a hand grenade had gone off in them,' O'Donovan explains. 'There were people who'd glued dentures in with superglue, stuck needles into an abscess to get rid of an infection, and one guy who could get on to a drug treatment programme if he was clean but his toothache was so bad he was using drugs to self-medicate.'

Over six months, operating one night a week, the Dewsbury project treated 170 patients – sometimes 12–14 in a night. One of the early ones was Clare Skipper, who turned up at the clinic to correct the mess she'd made when she pulled out her own tooth with a pair of pliers in her garden shed. She'd been in agony for weeks. 'It was excruciating – worse than labour pains,' she recalls. She'd tried to get an NHS dentist but nowhere was taking on new patients so she couldn't register, and she couldn't afford private treatment.

The only emergency clinic was in Bradford, which costs a fortune to get to on public transport. Her dad was also suffering from toothache, so they met in her garden shed, drank whisky and pulled their teeth out with pliers. Her dad managed to get his out but Clare's broke – the pain was indescribable. A week later, she walked into the Real Tooth Project where a dentist removed what was left. 'No one in

Britain should have to resort to pulling out their own teeth,'
she insists. 'And after all that I'm still not able to register with
a dentist and I dread something going wrong with my teeth
again.' She can't afford the £30 a month required to go on a
private care plan – she sometimes barely has enough money
for the electricity meter.

'Everything that we started to see here in the UK, I have
been seeing in Africa for the last twenty-five years,' says Ian
Wilson, one of DentAid's dentists. People are self-medicating, they get their mate to get them some antibiotics or use
some antibiotics left in their cupboard when they had a chest
infection. That's a common theme. Lots of DIY – I'll take
this bugger out, because I can't afford the £50. Dose yourself
up and sit through and ride this thing out. Some go to accident and emergency (A&E) and let them sort it out which
means A&E just gets absolutely swamped with inappropriate walk-ins. The one thing we're not seeing yet is the quack
healer – the witch doctor – but I wouldn't be surprised.'

Wilson points out that, while they were removing teeth
with terrible problems, to bring patients mouths up to normal
standards is effectively impossible under the current NHS
dental funding system. Traditionally dentists were paid by
the job – you see somebody, they need six fillings, you do the
six fillings, you get paid for six fillings. In 2006, however, a
new dental contract reorganised this structure – dentists were
given a specific number of Units of Dental Activity (UDAs),
effectively units of payment worth between £15 and £25
depending on the local Primary Care Trust. If a dentist does
a simple course of treatment, they earn 1 UDA, fillings or
extractions earn 3 UDAs, and a course of treatment that needs
lab work like dentures or crowns earns 12 UDAs. However,

the UDA simply pays for the overall treatment – so a dentist gets 12 UDAs, or roughly £180, for doing a crown. It doesn't matter if it is one crown or twenty crowns, the dentist only gets paid 12 UDAs. If a dentist does root work they get 3 UDAs, or £45. It doesn't matter if it is a simple upper incisor, or five difficult molars – the payment is the same.

To fix up poor-quality mouths as seen in Dewsbury, it might take anything up to eight hours – for the same fee as a one-filling job. As a result, NHS dentists are reluctant to take on longer courses of treatment. Wilson explains: 'So what started to happen was that dentists were looking at those people who were in high needs areas or high need or high demand and thinking – I'm not going to do all of that. I'm going to do one tooth and send them away. Basically, it was supervised neglect and, to a degree, it is still one of the problems within the current contract, where people just aren't getting the treatment done that they sadly need because it's financially impossible.'

The resulting imbalance in the UK's oral health is stark. Research published in the *Journal of Dental Research* in 2014 found that poorer Brits have, on average, eight fewer teeth – a quarter of a full adult set – than the richest by the time they reach their seventies. Dr Patricia Lucas, at Bristol University's school for policy studies, has been studying data from the city's dental hospital which shows children from disadvantaged backgrounds are significantly more likely to have early tooth decay and to need teeth extracted under general anaesthetic. In 2013 – the most recent data available – 721 children had decaying teeth extracted under general anaesthetic, and 155 of those children were under five. The majority were from poorer wards in the city – Bristol South, Ashley and Lawrence Hill.

'For those kids it's yet another hurdle they'll struggle to overcome if they're going to claw their way out of poverty,' Lucas explained. 'There's research from the US that shows poor teeth hinder your chances of getting a job and getting married – the two fundamentals for building a stable life.'

The inequality of access to care is similar when it comes to basic GP provision. In Scotland, despite wide differences in health needs, the general practice workforce is flatly distributed, so the areas of most need are not being serviced by enough doctors. In England, the Centre for Workforce Intelligence estimates that – in terms of GP coverage and deprivation – the poorest quintile of the population has fewer GPs (62.5 per 100,000) than the richest quintile (76.2 per 100,000).

Research carried out by the Royal College of General Practitioners in 2014 showed that people living in the most deprived communities face the longest waiting times – 22 per cent of people in Bradford struggled to make an appointment with their GP while the figure was just 5 per cent in Bath and northeast Somerset. North, east and west Devon have sixty GPs for every 100,000 patients – three times as many as Slough in Berkshire which has just twenty-two. Eight out of ten areas with the longest GP waiting times have moderate to high levels of deprivation.

Sheena, a part-time cleaner and mother of two, was struck down by a debilitating condition at the start of 2015 – she was exhausted and was throwing up every morning, her muscles ached and she was running a high fever. She had very little money left on her pay-as-you-go phone, but rang the surgery at 8.30 am and was kept on hold until the money ran out. 'You can't always afford to top the mobile phones up,' she explains. 'Quite a lot of what I earn goes on that. Electricity is more important; gas is more important; food is more important. Paying my rent is more important – I don't smoke, I don't drink. I don't buy clothes. I struggle with swimming lessons, I struggle to pay bus fares, I struggle to make the month meet. And then I had to text people and ask them to phone the doctor for me, do you know what I mean?'

In the end she went to A&E, where they diagnosed Lyme disease, a bacterial infection spread by a tick bite.

'GPs don't allow walk-in appointments anymore – round here and pretty much everywhere else,' Richardson explains. 'Some people we work with only have pay-as-you-go phones – if they run out of money, they can't make calls or access their answerphone. They have to wait till the community centre is open at 9.30 am to use the phone, by which time all the appointments have gone. Sometimes they feel embarrassed to fill out the free prescription form and prefer to get help from friends who don't judge them as scroungers. People will maybe take half a course of a drug and keep some of them in case something comes back. If one of the neighbours or friends needs them, they'll help out.'

In evidence to Parliament in 2006, the National Association of Citizens Advice Bureaux estimated that around 750,000 people fail to get their prescriptions dispensed because of cost. Doctors, nurses and pharmacists reported patients asking if all the medicines prescribed were really necessary as they couldn't afford to pay for every one.

But health inequality runs still deeper in the UK. In 2010 Professor Sir Michael Marmot published the Marmot Review – the findings of a long study by a team of medical experts into health inequality. He found that, in England, people living in the poorest neighbourhoods died, on average, seven years earlier than people in the richest neighbourhoods. Taking a tram across Manchester from Rochdale town centre to Timperley would add an extra twelve years to a man's life and seven years to a woman's life.

Even more disturbing, the average difference in disability-free life expectancy is seventeen years – meaning people in poorer areas not only die sooner, but spend more of their shorter lives with a disability. Even excluding the poorest 5 per cent and the richest 5 per cent, Marmot found the gap in life expectancy between low and high income was six years, and in disability-free life expectancy thirteen years.

This concept of a disability-free life has been politicised since the Thatcher government started issuing unemployed ex-miners and steelworkers incapacity benefit in the 1980s. Between 1979 and 1995 the numbers claiming the benefit jumped from 600,000 to 1.5 million. In 2013 even the Conservative chancellor, George Osborne, accused the Thatcher and Major governments of 'quick-fix politics of the worst kind' that 'parked' people on disability benefits.

The Work Capability Assessment (WCA) – initially introduced by the Labour government in 2008 but ramped up under the coalition – was designed to take people off them. The assessments – unlike earlier benefits that relied on a patient's GP – were carried out by computer, initially provided by French IT company Atos, which abandoned the contract in 2014, at which point it passed to MAXIMUS, a US healthcare data company.

Computer assessment has always been controversial. The film *I, Daniel Blake* tells the story of a fifty-nine-year-old man assessed fit to work despite having had a heart attack. There are many equivalent real-life examples. In 2012, Paul Turner died from ischaemic heart disease after being told he wasn't eligible for Employment and Support Allowance. In 2013, David Duncan had his Jobseeker's Allowance withheld when he failed to attend his Jobcentre appointment after suffering a major cardiac arrest two days earlier. In 2014, Oldham East and Saddleworth MP Debbie Abrahams told the story of one of her constituents who had a heart attack during his WCA assessment and was later sanctioned because he had 'withdrawn from the assessment'. In March 2016, figures from the DWP showed more than half the disabled people declared fit to work have the assessment overturned on appeal.

These brutal assessments, that campaigners claim have led to the deaths of around a hundred people, are driven by the austerity cuts. In 2011, the DWP forecast that the numbers on incapacity benefit would come down by 16.5 per cent, or 0.5 million, as a result of the WCA, saving £3.5 billion a year in 2014–15. And yet, those savings have not materialised – and only 5 per cent of people have moved into work. To compensate, from April 2017 new ESA claimants will receive the same money as those on Jobseeker's Allowance or Universal Credit.

Marmot didn't avoid the cost implications of health inequality, but he decided it made sound financial sense to tackle it. He estimated that the cost of treating the various illnesses that result from inequalities in obesity alone was £2 billion per year. He estimated that inequality in illness accounts for productivity losses of £32 billion per year. The overall cost of health inequality over five years was roughly £350 billion.

Beveridge would have approved of this cost analysis – his reasons for recommending the formation of the health service were almost brutally practical. Regarding an NHS paid for by National Insurance contributions, he explained, 'Disease and accidents must be paid for in any case, in lessened power of production and in idleness, if not directly by insurance benefits. It is preferable to pay for disease and accident openly and directly in the form of insurance benefits, rather than indirectly, as this emphasises the cost and should give a stimulus to prevention.'

Marmot updated his report in 2015 with findings that just under a quarter of English households don't earn enough to live healthily – an increase from 20 per cent in 2008. Hull, Derby, Westminster, Middlesbrough and Nottingham had seen the largest increase in deprivation, although encouragingly Waltham Forest, the Isles of Scilly, Greenwich, Hackney and Newham saw the largest decreases in deprivation. The average man in Blackpool – the poorest neighbourhood – could expect to live fifty-five years without disability. Meanwhile in Wokingham, the richest neighbourhood, he would, on average, reach the age of seventy-one – a difference of more than sixteen years.

This is particularly unfair on children – if you're born into a low-income household, the chances are you'll be sicker and weaker and die sooner than most of the population. Childhood mortality (deaths between birth and the age of fourteen) in the UK is significantly higher than similar countries in Europe – only Poland, Hungary, Malta, Slovakia and Latvia have higher child mortality rates. In children under five, the UK mortality rate is the highest in Western Europe, double that of Sweden.

Infant mortality is strongly linked to poverty and material deprivation – there is a fivefold difference in infant mortality rates between the lowest and highest socio-economic groups. Professor Marmot concluded that one-quarter of all deaths under the age of one year would potentially be avoided if all births had the same level of risk as for women with the lowest level of deprivation, and that eliminating child poverty in the UK would save the lives of 1,400 children under fifteen years of age annually.

Marmot also described the economic advantages of equal opportunities for both rich and poor to enjoy good health. If everyone in England had the same death rates as the most advantaged, people who are currently dying prematurely as a result of health inequalities would, in total, have enjoyed between 1.3 and 2.5 million extra years of life. They would, in addition, have had a further 2.8 million years free of limiting illness or disability. Inequality in illness accounts for productivity losses of £31–3 billion per year, lost taxes and higher welfare payments in the range of £20–32 billion per year, and additional NHS healthcare costs associated with inequality are well in excess of £5.5 billion per year.

And this is money the NHS needs – the service is desperately strapped for cash as it struggles through its 'most austere decade ever', according to the King's Fund. Between 2009–10 and 2020–1, spending on the NHS in England will rise by just 0.9 per cent per year. This is leading to a lethal shortfall – in 2015–16, NHS trusts finished the year a record £2.45 billion in debt. In May 2016, the King's Fund surveyed NHS trust finance directors and more than half of the clinical commissioning groups' finance leads, and found two-thirds of them admitting that the quality of patient care in their area has deteriorated over the 2015–16 period. In November 2016, a BBC freedom of information (FOI) request showed ambulance response times in England, Scotland and Northern Ireland were increasing – one-third of ambulances fail to meet targets for life-threatening callouts.

With more than 13,000 beds closed in 2016 and over-seventy-fives turning up in A&E due to social care cuts of £5 billion, 8 per cent of patients – more than 1.85 million people – spent longer than four hours in A&E across the year, the highest number since 2003–4. At the end of March 2016, the number of patients waiting for hospital treatment stood at 3.7 million – up 17 per cent, or almost 500,000 patients, over the year.

In August 2016, the BBC reported on NHS England's draft sustainability and transformation plans which proposed ward closures, cuts in bed numbers and changes to A&E and GP care in forty-four areas in a bid to meet Treasury demands for £22 billion in efficiency savings by 2020. In January 2017, the government announced cuts to the NHS budget of 0.6 per cent per person in 2018–19.

As a result, DentAid is already being joined by other developing world charities to help prop up our ailing healthcare system. Doctors of the World is an international NGO that runs a primary care clinic for migrants in Bethnal Green and Brighton while, in January 2017, the Red Cross deployed teams at a number of hospitals in the East Midlands to provide ambulances and help deal with patients left lying on trolleys, with Red Cross chief executive Mike Adamson warning of an impending 'humanitarian crisis in our hospital and ambulance services across the country'.

That crisis is already here. In Leicester I met Mark, a long-term homeless *Big Issue* vendor. Mark is in his mid-forties, but with stretched skin and deep bags under his eyes that make him look older. He used to live with his mother, he explains, and loved doing chores with her. After she died, he went a little downhill – he drank more and started mixing with a crowd of heavy drug users. Suspecting him of dealing, the police broke down his door in a dawn raid and tore the place apart. They couldn't find any drugs or drug paraphernalia but took a few expensive-looking items of clothing, like his leather jacket, which they accused him of stealing. He hadn't, he insists – still outraged. He'd got them from the Littlewoods catalogue.

'If they'd broken my door down and found nothing they'd have to pay to repair it, but because they said they found stolen gear, they could refuse,' Mark explains. He didn't have the money to fix the door right away, and in the few days before he could get started, 'my so-called friends just walked in and took all my tools'.

He ended up in a tent in a small park near Leicester's town centre, drinking heavily. In the winter of 2015–16 the first finger on his right hand started to turn black – shooting little veins of darkness down the skin. Then his index finger started to blacken. He tried picking the black lines out with a pin, trying to root them out from his skin – 'or I'd have lost my hand', he explains. The black – gangrene – continued to spread and one night he got very drunk and chopped the end of the fingers off just below the first knuckle.

To deal with incidents like this the Bradford-based homeless GP practice, Bevan Healthcare, operates a street medicine team run by one doctor and one nurse from a cross between an ambulance and a converted motorhome. They arrive at certain food banks, soup kitchens and, in some cases, car parks. The team arrive in one car park at night – people emerge from the darkness, receive treatment and disappear again. Among other things, they're treating rising numbers of people with severe malnutrition.

Oxfam and Church Action on Poverty estimate that 2 million people in the UK are malnourished, with 3 million at risk of becoming so. Thirty-six per cent of the UK population are just one heating bill or a broken washing machine away from hardship and one in six parents have gone without food themselves in order to feed their families. According to the Department of Health, people with malnutrition accounted for 184,528 hospital bed days in 2015, and mortality figures from the ONS showing 391 people dying from malnutrition or hunger over the year – up 27 per cent from 2006–7. Shockingly, this means thirty-two people starve to death in the UK every month, or one person every day.

Food banks and homeless charities have been spotting growing signs of malnutrition over the past four years. The UK's largest food bank, the Trussell Trust, deals with 'parents who go hungry so their children can have enough to eat every day', according to the Trust's food bank network director Adrian Curtis. Pensioners and younger single people are also going hungry – like twenty-one-year-old Charlotte who was funding herself through college, working two evening jobs until she was made redundant from both jobs within a month, leaving her unable to afford food. When she arrived at the Trust's food bank she was dehydrated and in the first stages of malnutrition.

Between April and September 2016, the Trust's 429 food banks distributed 519,342 three-day emergency food supplies to people in crisis – up from 506,369 during the same period last year – with 188,584 going to children.

Since the Trust's food bank network started in 2004, some things have remained constant, says Curtis. 'The primary reason people are referred to us is benefit issues – benefit delays, benefit changes, and sanctions,' he explains. 'There's also been a steady increase in people referred to us while they're in work – with low pay or insecure employment.'

From April to September 2016, 27.45 per cent of referrals were due to benefit delays, while 24.9 per cent were down to low income while in work. 'It's usually when a crisis arrives – a large bill, a problem with the car, the boiler goes wrong,' he explains. 'People don't have the money to deal with it so they have to choose between paying the bill and putting food on the table.'

Food bank referrals can make for heart-breaking reading. One from a North Lanarkshire agency, in March 2015, reads, 'This is a referral for a vulnerable lone parent . . . I have referred her previously due to a mix up with child tax credits. She has three children – youngest son just discharged from hospital after surgery to remove brain tumour and have stent fitted. Mum failed to attend Jobcentre when son was in hospital. Access to food bank would alleviate stress for this Family.'

The Trust usually finds people only need one or two interventions in a six-month period. In Dundee, however, it's helping forty-something Paul Jenkins who was sanctioned for an astonishing three years for failing to show evidence of ten job searches a week, for being ten minutes late for an appointment and for claiming that having no phone or computer made it hard to conduct meaningful job searches in a city with the fourth-worst employment rate in the UK.

Paul was a chef at the Hilton Hotel until it was demolished in 2014 to make way for a new waterfront development. Since being sanctioned he's survived on a hardship allowance of £36 a week – or £5.14 per day, out of which he has to pay for water, electricity and gas bills as well as food, clothes and transport until September 2018. Although most Trussell Trust users are one-offs, the Dundee branch had given Paul eleven packages of essentials by March 2016, so extreme was his need.

'People should not need to rely on food aid in one of the wealthiest countries in the world,' says Curtis. 'That should not become the new norm. We are very keen not to replace the welfare system – we don't want to see people go hungry in our country and we hope food banks aren't a permanent feature. There are so many stereotypes and so much rhetoric about the undeserving poor – but if policymakers just went to food banks and met the people who need emergency food, they'd find that none of them are scroungers. Late benefit delivery, unfair sanctions, low pay, insecure employment – these are not their fault. Food aid is short-term relief. Communities suffering long-term entrenched poverty have major structural factors keeping them down – higher rates of low-paying work, lower educational attainment rates and a shortage of jobs. Unless we tackle these things, malnutrition isn't going away.'

Even in the 1940s, Beveridge didn't list hunger as one of the Five Giants that needed to be slain.

4

Idleness

Of all the want shown by the surveys, from three-quarters to five-sixths was due to interruption or loss of earning power . . .

Most men who have once gained the habit of work would rather work – in ways to which they are used – than be idle, and all men would rather be well than ill.

Sir William Beveridge, *Social Insurance and Allied Services Report*

Over the summer of 2016 I took a receptionist's job at one of the Leicester branches of ManpowerGroup – a US multinational 'human resource consulting' firm, based in Milwaukee, although the vast majority of its business is in Europe. In 2015, ManpowerGroup made profits of $690 million on revenues of $19.3 billion worldwide.

I'd previously worked as an office temp for Manpower, as it was then known, while trying to find my first full-time job. When I arrived at the Leicester office in 2016, however, it was clear things had changed. The branch split the business between office admin jobs and warehouse jobs, picking and packing to fulfil customer orders in a string of warehouses some distance outside town. Leicester – and Leicestershire – has huge numbers of giant warehouses with constantly fluctuating employment needs, I was told.

My job was to be at the front desk, where I was to ask new people walking in what they were looking for. People came in every day; maybe five people a day signed up in the office but not all of them got put through to the next stage. The main thing that discounted people was transport: the warehouses were in the middle of nowhere, almost impossible to get to by public transport. If you didn't have a car or know someone who worked there with a car, you couldn't work.

Most of the walk-ins came early. The afternoon was spent handling the phone-around frenzy that began at 3.00 pm when every warehouse would ring in its orders for the following day: we need twelve people tomorrow, we need thirty tomorrow, we need thirty-eight tomorrow.

Once the orders came in, we'd start ringing all the people on the books, offering the rate, the address and the hours with the key question: 'Can you be there on time?' At the same time, there would be a series of calls from warehouse pickers and packers desperate for work.

Through my entire time there, speaking to countless people, not one British-born person signed up for any of these jobs, or was even on the books. If there had been Brits, they would have been in high demand: warehouses kept requesting English speakers but we usually couldn't supply them.

I asked the woman who'd given me the job why there were so many Eastern Europeans – did the agency have a policy? Were there deals in place? She briefly looked around to see if anyone was listening and said, 'Look at the conditions, the pay and the hours – they're so shit. No one else wants these jobs.'

That seemed partly true: the conditions were terrible, usually involving searches and no guarantees of work at all. If you were trying to raise a family or build a life, there was no guarantee of work or money, and you might lose a job simply because the staff were in a bad mood with you that day.

One senior manager would cross names off the ring-around list if they annoyed her for any reason – especially if they had time off sick or couldn't make a booking. Sometimes staff decided not to give someone work for two or three days to punish them for some transgression. They were just dealing with people as commodities. There was never a discussion as to whether they needed the work or were relying on the work. Just a black mark they'd never understand.

And the pay – for those who got the work – was minimum wage, sometimes with deductions that were never entirely clear. I'd often have to put people through who had phoned to complain that they hadn't been paid the right money. Manpower received almost double the amount for every worker they supplied, but companies were willing to pay a little extra to ensure daily flexibility and a complete absence of any employer responsibility for sick pay or redundancy.

Workers also had to pay for their own transport. Manpower might corral a worker with a car into picking up a group, but if they got a lift they had to pay, and it could end up costing an hour or two in wages. Some people were only working perhaps one day a week, and it was hard to see how they could afford to pay any rent. Inclusion Healthcare, Leicester's GP practice that serves the homeless, says the numbers of Eastern Europeans sleeping rough has been increasing for the past couple of years.

Most of the walk-ins were word-of-mouth recommendations. Nine out of ten knew someone who worked through Manpower already. Sometimes you'd find whole families looking for work there. The recommendation usually came from one of the small number of regular workers who were given enough hours to live on and treated comparatively well. These were all workers who could drive, had reasonable English, turned up every day and were available at short notice. Because the work was so sporadic, people dropped off the books regularly and there was constant turnover. Sometimes staff were so desperate for workers that they'd fill in application forms for people and put other workers down as referees.

I got to know one worker – Alby, a middle-aged father of two with debts that were constantly stressing him out. If he hadn't heard from anyone by 3.30 pm, he'd be calling to see if anything was going. It usually wasn't. Alby was second tier: he'd probably get work if something was available. Once I had to call him at 9.00 am and tell him he was needed in forty-five minutes. His phone, he told me, runs his life. And I was unusual in calling him; mostly people just text, he said. His dream was a permanent job, he said, but he didn't know anyone who had made that jump.

One day, he got a black mark as he had failed to accept a job. He phoned in the afternoon and the following morning, the following afternoon and, presumably, the following day. My five days were over. I left the agency and didn't speak to him before I went.

Employment agencies have a long history. As far back as the 1920s some were supplying short-term contract workers for a one-off fee. In the 1950s, agencies began hiring out staff to firms on a temporary basis in return for a mark-up on the workers' hourly wage. This activity was concentrated in London, usually in clerical and secretarial occupations. The agencies tended to be small businesses, operating on a local or regional level. From 1973 to 1994, employment agencies were governed by a licensing regime introduced by the Conservative MP Kenneth Lewis. Under the system, agencies required a licence to operate that could be revoked if they failed certain basic standards. In 1994, the Conservative MP John Redwood passed the Deregulation and Contracting Out Act, which removed the need for licences or, indeed, any other regulation for agencies.

As a result the industry changed shape, leading to the growth of multinational firms that managed long-term supply contracts from companies to provide large numbers of temps on a quasi-continuous basis. Many contracts – like Amazon's contract with Randstad to handle recruitment, shift patterns, warehouse floor management and pay at their UK warehouses – involve the agency undertaking a full spectrum of human resources activities, from payroll management to contracts and training. In these large contracts, temps are often seen as 'permanent temps', undertaking core roles in the client firms where they are working.

Analysis of the Labour Force Survey by the Resolution Foundation shows that there are an estimated 865,000 agency workers in the UK today. This means agency workers are as significant a group in numerical terms as the 900,000 working on zero-hours contracts. And the number of agency workers has risen by over 200,000 since 2011 – the equivalent of a 30 per cent increase over the period, while the number on zero-hours contracts rose 20 per cent from 2015 to 2016.

The fragmenting and casualisation of work is taking many forms – from part-time work (IFS data released in January 2017 showed a fourfold increase in low-paid men working part-time – one in five compared with one in twenty in 1996) to the so-called gig economy. Agency work, however, is the only one that's mandatory – anyone signing on at a Jobcentre must also sign up with two agencies as a condition of receiving benefit. Perhaps the most infamous result of this rise is the relationship between high street retailer Sports Direct and the agencies Transline and Best Connection to run its warehouse in Shirebrook.

Shirebrook is a once-prosperous former mining town in Derbyshire now littered with shops and pubs that have been shuttered or lie empty, leaving takeaway restaurants, charity shops, tanning salons and a Polish delicatessen or two. The local colliery opened in 1896 and closed in 1993, with the loss of 1,400 jobs. When Mike Ashley opened the Sports Direct warehouse on the site of the pit in 2005, the *Independent* ran a breathless profile:

> the swanky facility . . . bears a close resemblance to the interior of an
> elite US athletics academy . . . Shirebrook is likely to remain in the

retail sector's winning circle for the foreseeable future. This is a prospect few miners could have envisaged when the colliery closed in 1993.

And, yet, former miners make up a tiny fraction of the warehouse workforce.

Sports Direct pays an estimated £50 million per year to two agencies – Transline and Best Connection – to supply and manage over 3,000 warehouse staff. Transline, in particular, has an interesting history. There are still some areas of agency work that face regulation. In 2004, some twenty-one Chinese cockle pickers drowned in Morecambe Bay when they were cut off by the rising tide, and the following year the Gangmasters Licensing Authority (GLA) was founded. This institution licenses agencies working in agriculture, dairy farming, gathering shellfish and almost every other part of growing, collecting and packaging food.

In 2006, Qualitycourse Ltd, of Halifax Road, Brighouse – part of the Transline Group – secured a GLA licence to supply temporary workers to a factory in Bolton, which makes own-brand pizzas for Britain's biggest retailers. In 2013, the licence lapsed and the company reapplied – stating that it turned over £1 million in the food sector. The GLA began an inspection of Transline's employment practices and 'throughout the subsequent inspection process, the business was obstructive and proved reluctant to provide any information about its operations under the lapsed licence', according to a GLA statement issued in 2014.

When the GLA inspectors called they found Transline running a salary sacrifice scheme, paying workers partly in expenses and partly in wages – Transline, the GLA concluded, was likely not to be paying 'adequate tax and

National Insurance contributions'. The GLA reviewed a sample of payslips and found that some workers were receiving much less than the national minimum wage, 'some . . . significantly so'. One worker was paid just £2.87 an hour before expenses. Transline claimed the low-paid employees were apprentices, but the GLA found the 'workers interviewed did not consider they were employed as apprentices'. The GLA ruled that Transline had failed its licensing standard by not paying the national minimum wage, and found Transline's managing directors, Paul Beaseley and Jon Taylor, not 'fit and proper' persons to hold a GLA licence.

In 2013, the GLA terminated Transline's licence to operate in the food industry in any capacity. Despite having its licence revoked, Transline carried on supplying workers illegally for a period in late summer 2013. The GLA ruling had no effect on Transline's other business. It continues to manage warehouses for the likes of ASOS and Amazon, including Amazon's Dunfermline warehouse, where pickers and packers in orange vests push trolleys around at the behest of satnav computers telling them where to walk next and what to pick up when they get there, while the devices measure their speed and productivity in real time. Employees regularly camp close to the warehouse by the M90 to ensure they arrive on time, fearful of severe penalties for being late.

At Sports Direct's Shirebrook warehouse, the staff are almost exclusively Eastern European workers, imported by and for the agencies. Transline's Polish branch, Transline Polska, promises accommodation and transport to and from work as part of its recruitment drive, using an EU scheme for relocation costs worth £727 through EURES, the European Employment Services. In some cases, the recruitment was unethical; in others, downright illegal. In January 2017, Erwin Markowski and his brother Krystian were jailed under slavery legislation for trafficking Polish men to work for Transline at Shirebrook. The duo employed a spotter in Poland who identified people prepared to travel to the UK on the promise of work. The brothers took their passports, opened bank accounts for them and withdrew most of their income. They put the men up in cramped red-brick houses – usually ten men to a house – and charged them for everything.

For those not enslaved by traffickers, conditions are still bleak. One local cab firm had the pick-up job for new workers in the early years. Until 2015, they'd drive a minibus to Birmingham to something called the 'holding farm' – a huge field full of static caravans at the end of a country lane. They'd pick up groups of silent men and take them to a large house near the Shirebrook Miners Welfare Centre, then pick them up again the following morning and drive them to Chesterfield to sign on with one of the agencies.

Agency workers are either on zero-hours contracts or so-called '336' contracts, meaning a guaranteed 336 hours' work over a twelve-month period. In practice this means that a worker delivering forty hours a week loses their rights to ongoing weekly hours and associated payments roughly nine weeks into the year. This effectively leaves them on zero-hours contracts and allows anyone, from management to line supervisors, to dismiss them without pay.

Talking to one Polish worker at a social event in the Shirebrook Miners Welfare Centre, he explained what that meant: 'There's no disciplinary process – it's complete control over you,' he said, slowly sipping a Coke. 'If they don't like you, they don't like a comment that you make or you're sick once too often . . . whatever it might be, they don't have to put you through a disciplinary process or anything. They just simply tell you, "Sorry we've got no more hours for you." There's no appeal against that.'

In 2015, two undercover reporters from the *Guardian* were smuggled into the warehouse for day shifts and reported scenes of Dickensian misery. The Shirebrook shifts started at 5.30 am. Cars packed with Eastern European workers dropped people off at the huge, brightly lit warehouse – its 800,000 square feet looming like an invading Martian spaceship at the end of a country lane. Staff filed in under surveillance cameras carrying their packed lunches in transparent bags – everything was subject to search, and even wearing branded clothing, a rule breaker, was enough to get people pulled out of line.

The main warehouse – 2,000 feet long and 400 feet wide – is filled with long, blue shelves tapering off into the distance. Standing at one end, it's almost impossible to see the wall at the other side. The racks of shelves are stacked four high on the top floor, just under the overhanging roof, and almost fifty feet high in the larger ground-floor space. The aisles are narrow, often littered with boxes. There are no windows – bright white arc lights give everything an unreal quality.

Staff cover some twenty miles every day inside the warehouse, with sheets listing the products they need to fetch and stack in a webbing and metal trolley, trying to hit targeted finishing times – which usually require running down the narrow aisles. Tasks are tiring and repetitive: from shelf-stacking to gathering items and covering them in polythene covers. Managers monitor performance with fastest and slowest league tables published outside the staff canteen. Staff are constantly observed from on high. Slow movers are called out by name on a speaker system and urged to hurry up.

At the time of the *Guardian* investigation, Transline used a 'strike system' – a list of offences punishable by a strike against employee names, published weekly on the Transline noticeboards. Six strikes in a six-month period meant instant dismissal. Among the possible offences Transline listed were time-wasting, excessive chatting, long toilet breaks, poor housekeeping, being late in or early out, unexplained dead time and periods of reported sickness.

In effect, talking to anyone else meant a strike. One day sick meant a strike. Taking a day off to look after their children – strike. Local primary schools complained about sick children being dropped off at school by mums who had to work – schools were unable to contact parents to get permission to give medicine or report a deterioration in the child. Nine-year-old kids would go home after school, find their parents still working and return to school because they had nowhere else to go.

There were no first aid kits and few trained first aiders. Safety rules were widely flouted – with crowded aisles, defective equipment and products stacked dangerously high. FOI requests to the Bolsover Council and East Midlands Ambulance service revealed a total of 110 ambulances or paramedic cars called out to the warehouse between 1 January 2013 and 19 April 2016 – with fifty cases classified as 'life threatening', including chest pain, breathing problems, convulsions, fitting and strokes, while other incidents included the amputation of a finger down to the first knuckle, a fractured neck, crushed hand and numerous smaller hand, wrist, back and head injuries.

Twelve of these incidents were listed as 'major' injuries – with seventy-nine injuries leading to absences from work of over seven days. Staff were three times more likely to be injured working at Shirebrook than in agriculture – statistically the most dangerous industry in the UK.

Shockingly, the ambulance service received five calls about women suffering pregnancy difficulties. In January 2014, an ambulance was called to the site to help a twenty-eight-year-old woman who had given birth in the staff toilets at the site. She had gone to work despite being heavily pregnant – afraid of losing her job. After giving birth, she tried to go back to work. Ambulance staff told the police, who then arrested her for wilful neglect.

The *Guardian* reporters found many of the workers had been employed for more than a year, with some having been on an agency contract for over six years under the continuous promise of being made permanent. None had made it. Both agencies made deductions for 'insurance services' from employee pay – ranging from 45p to £2.45 a week. Employees without a bank account were charged a £10 one-off fee for a pre-paid debit card on to which their wages were paid. A management fee of £10 per month was deducted from these cards, as well as 75p for cash withdrawals and 10p for a text notifying transactions, while a paper statement cost £1.50.

They also suffered deductions from their wage packets for clocking in for a shift a minute late. These practices contributed to many being paid an effective rate of about £6.50 an hour against the then statutory minimum wage rate of £6.70, saving the firm millions of pounds a year at the expense of some of the poorest workers in the UK.

At the end of a shift, after formally clocking off, staff had to line up for compulsory searches that could last anything between twenty-five and forty-five minutes, all the while unpaid. The searches could be humiliating – some female workers were told to drop their trousers or lift their skirts. Some women were offered more and regular shifts in exchange for sexual favours by particular supervisors.

These stories from Sports Direct are the tip of the iceberg. The only reason news of the warehouse conditions leaked out is down to the union Unite beginning a long, slow process of trying to organise the workforce. Similar conditions – with slight variations – are in place in warehouses across the country.

Short-hours contracts – like those at Sports Direct that offer a bare minimum of hours – are slowly taking over from zero-hours contracts, as firms look to avoid the poor publicity. Short-hours contracts, of course, aren't measured as zero hours and aren't advertised as zero hours, but offer so little guaranteed work that the effects are the same. Keeping hours down helps firms avoid paying National Insurance, which they have to do for every employee paid more than £155 per week.

In Stoke, Mark is on a four-hour contract with Kentucky Fried Chicken. He had been led to believe that the four-hour minimum was purely admin and more hours would be the norm. After six weeks of working four hours every week and earning just under £30, he was desperate to shift to McDonalds, he explained, because they offer thirty-five hours. A *Sunday Mirror* survey of jobs advertised by major retail chains in 2004 found that Argos and Homebase offered contracts as short as three hours a week. Tesco's shortest contracts were just 3.5 hours. The Arcadia group – which includes Dorothy Perkins, Miss Selfridge, Topman and Topshop – offered four-hour contracts, while Curry's, PC World and Next guaranteed six hours per week.

At minimum wage rates (outside London) of £5.60 per hour for those under twenty-one, £7.05 per hour for people aged between twenty-one and twenty-four and £7.50 for over twenty-fives, that means a guaranteed salary of £16–33 per week, £21–42.30 per week and £22–45 per week respectively. Staff interviewed by the *Sunday Mirror* told of people desperately waiting for a call or text offering extra shifts, or even queuing up for them. One Tesco worker, a mother-of-one, from Cottingham, East Riding, reported, 'Notices go up offering the extra hours available and there's always a raft of people waiting to sign. It's on a first-come, first-served basis so there's a bit of rivalry to get on the list. Occasionally, we might get a text offering us more hours.'

The Resolution Foundation's agency research also compared the pay of zero-hours and non-zero-hours workers doing similar jobs across five years from 2011 to 2016, using Labour Force Survey (LFS) statistics on salary, and found that workers on zero-hours contracts face a 'precarious pay penalty' of almost 7 per cent – or £1,000 a year for a typical worker. Compensating for differences in gender, age, experience, qualification level, occupation, industry and length of service, the LFS numbers show zero-hours workers typically earn 93p an hour, or 6.6 per cent, less than their exact equivalents on full-time contracts. For someone working twenty-one hours a week, this amounts to £1,000 a year.

For lower-paying roles, the lowest 20 per cent of earners on zero-hours contracts face a penalty of at least 9.5 per cent.

Temporary workers suffer a 5.5 per cent penalty and permanent agency workers take a 2.4 per cent, or £430, hit. The great defence of zero-hours contracts is flexibility for staff and employer. These pay penalties show they also hold down wages.

In Shirebrook I met Andy Phipps – a sixty-something former coal miner and subsequently warehouse worker. He worked at the coalface in Shirebrook pit, then as a picker and packer for DHL. The pit, he recalls, was dangerous and dirty – 'Depending on depth, pits are either too cold or too warm,' he explains. 'Shirebrook was sub-tropical. But there was a camaraderie. You were all working together – taking it on as a team. At the warehouse I worked alone all day long – just moving stuff about. It was heavy lifting but not as hard as the coalface. It was just isolating.'

He said that back in the late nineteenth and early twentieth century, Shirebrook pit had someone called the Butty Man. The Butty Man acted like an agency – the miners were directly employed by him, not the pit. Every Friday, he'd have 'the reckoning', where the men who worked for him met in a pub and he'd dish out the cash from a tin. 'We're going back to those days if we're not careful,' Phipps shook his head slowly. 'We're heading back to Victorian times.'

5

The New Full Employment

Full employment does not mean literally no unemployment; that is to say, it does not mean that every man and woman in the country who is fit and free for work is employed productively every day of his or her working life . . . Full employment means that unemployment is reduced to short intervals of standing by, with the certainty that very soon one will be wanted in one's old job again or will be wanted in a new job that is within one's powers.

Sir William Beveridge, *Full Employment in a Free Society*

Over Christmas 2016–17, Scott and Jordan, aged twenty-four and twenty-three, were picking and packing in a warehouse operated by DHL for the food giant Nisa, which supplies 2,500 independently owned grocers, including family-run corner stores, small chains like Loco and its own branded shops. DHL runs distribution for Nisa, but outsources its warehouse recruitment and employment to the agency Blue Arrow, which hit the headlines in 2014 for taking £2.50 per week from temporary workers' pay packets to cover accident insurance, when the market rate for such insurance was as low as 3p.

Nisa/DHL/Blue Arrow's huge warehouse in Stoke looks after chilled and frozen foods, so Scott and Jordan were in effect working in a giant freezer. They were given thick thermal overalls, thick boots and a headset that covered both ears, allowing controllers to issue orders telling them where to go, how many items to pick and where to take them. 'They'll give us a certain destination and then we'll weave in and out and get there, then get off the trucks to get the product and put it on to a pallet,' Scott explains. 'You're talking 25-kilo boxes, sometimes 30 kilos. There was one we had – that thing was 75 kilograms and it took two hours to actually put it on the pallet and they're yelling at you to hurry up over the headphones. I'm surprised I only had one injury at DHL – it was a 35-kilogram box but we didn't know what's inside. Some of them don't have the name of the item on them. I went to put the box on the pallet and my arm just gave way. All they said was 'Well we can wrap it up but we will have to send you home and we need a doctor's note if you don't come in tomorrow.' But it costs £7 for a doctor's note and you miss a day to go and get it so I just stayed on.'

At some point over the holiday season Jordan developed an infection in his foot. The boots they were given were lined with fur and the heavy work made him break out in a sweat. His socks and his skin were soaking for most of a shift. He was limping everywhere – his worried supervisor made him sign a piece of paper saying he was fit enough to work. 'Do you lie about it, say you're fit and keep your hours or put yourself in danger?' he shrugs. 'It's one of the things isn't it? I signed because I needed to be paid.'

When they first arrived they were told they would have a full-time job the following year if they impressed over Christmas. There was talk of a pension plan and holiday pay. Both were encouraged to find they were given a five-day training course in how to drive the electric order pickers – a cross between a manual pallet-lifter and a full fork-lift truck. 'You think to yourself "I've got this training so, yeah, they're definitely going to keep me on," ' Scott explains. 'So I set out to prove that I'm a good worker. You get twelve-hour shifts – some of them might be fifteen hours and you want to do that because you want to show that you're willing to work. We were doing stupid hours. If you got told to go home, we'll sit there and try and argue – saying, no we don't want to go home. I'll stay and do the work . . . but they'd send you home.'

Day shifts started at 7.00 am and night shifts at 7.00 pm. They'd clock in, and that's when their paid hours started. They had to swipe out for lunch break, which went unpaid, meaning a twelve-hour shift paid eleven hours. They could get sent home as soon as the work slacked off. On the night shifts, this could often be around 3.00 or 4.00 am. Public transport wasn't running and taking a car effectively erased a big chunk of their day's take, so they'd walk home in the small hours. 'The three days before Christmas they sent me home three days in a row at four o'clock in the morning,' Jordan explains ruefully. 'Full-time staff get first pick of the hours, and the agency can just pick and choose when they want you in. Agency staff are like basically disposable.'

Their shifts were erratic – one week Jordan worked seventy-two hours, the next week forty hours, then thirty-three hours, then eight. Everything was managed by text message. They'd get instructions by text at around 3.00 pm telling them if they were needed the following day or not. Sometimes there'd be a miscalculation – they'd go in and get sent home again, which cost them a £3.50 bus fare each way. Other times they'd get a text at 6.00 am saying they were needed the next day. They'd always say yes – those that didn't, didn't work.

Even their payslips came by text. They received no paper copies, just weekly texts telling them how many hours they'd worked and how much they were being paid. Jordan flicked through the texts to show me how it worked – one week he earned £102, the next week £70. With no payslip, it was impossible to determine what, if any, deductions had been made, but the salary divided by hours came in just under the minimum wage.

When they were both dropped by Blue Arrow immediately after Christmas, the text pay slips made it very tricky to claim housing benefit. The benefit office did not take them as proof of salary, and insisted on three pay slips to calculate how much they were allowed. Most of all, though, they were cross with themselves for having been taken in by the promise of a job. 'You hear the promises and you keep your hopes up and work till you're knackered out and as soon as we come to the new year, they sacked us off,' Jordan sighs. 'You'd been saying, yeah this could be a good opportunity. You're talking about it, you're thinking about it. You're making plans and whatnot and stuff like that and the next minute it doesn't happen. They're giving you so much hope it's unbelievable then they just drop you like a tonne of bricks. Why bullshit us? It runs you down – it really runs your body and your mind down. You get the job and you're willing and full of ideas and suggestions and then they drop you and you think – what's the point? It makes you want to give up.'

They've been struggling with their rent – it takes anything from two to six weeks to get housing and jobseeker benefits. 'And people go into this work trying to get something on their CVs but agency work is mixed jobs everywhere with no payslips for proof so employers look at your CV and think "What the hell is going on?" ' Scott explains. 'Every single agency that I've worked for gives me maximum two, two and a half months and they've cut me clean off.'

'It stresses you,' Jordan says. 'I worked with a lad at a warehouse a year ago who wanted to go out and sell himself, because he's scared of going homeless and you feel like your life's completely over. Every day when you're working for a zero contract, you're getting scared – because if you do a certain thing wrong then that's it. They cut you off. No money left in your bank, do you know what I mean? And you've got no money in your pocket and it scares you.'

Between the two of them, they've spent the last four or five years working on and off at warehouses for New Look and the luxury car company Bentley, as well as cleaning for an agency called RCB, and labouring for Network Rail. RCB gave Jordan jobs in Crewe, Petholme in Stoke and then back to Crewe on the same day, refusing to pay travel costs or for time travelling. Network Rail made them pay for their own training and insisted they pay the full train fare travelling from Stoke to Crewe.

Listening to them planning their working year is chilling. 'March to about the start of November you're getting six weeks here and eight weeks there, some holiday cover, that sort of thing,' Scott explains. 'You're basically waiting then until Christmas, which is when they need you the most. You try and save up some money so you can get a driving licence or make sure you've got the rent for two months. I'd love to get a passport to try for some summer work out in Spain, but they're £70/80.'

Jordan is hoping to start a plumbing course this year – he used to help his dad when he had plumbing work and knows how to handle most things, but without a qualification he can't get work. Scott is hoping for a job in McDonalds. 'Once you're in with McDonalds and you have passed that training period they guarantee you thirty-five hours a week,' he explains. 'And they look after you. People might take the mick with all the five-star badges and stuff but, to give you an example, McDonalds after ten years give all their managers a three-month sabbatical paid. They don't tell you that on the tin do you know what I mean? Once you're in . . .'

Facundo came to the UK from Spain in March 2014. He was driving for a wealthy Spanish family before then, but lost his job as the economy shrank. His first job was with online food delivery service EatFirst that paid him £4 per hour, with a £5 bonus for each delivery – drivers typically made two or three per shift, with shifts clustered around lunch and dinner. EatFirst provided his vehicle and he could earn up to £40 per day – which, with time off to visit his family in Spain, would deliver just under £10,000 per year.

He moved to Hermes, a service that considers all of its 10,500 couriers to be self-employed. Hermes couriers are paid per job, around 48p per parcel delivered. They have to provide their own transport, pay for fuel and car insurance, and are issued with a handset onto which they have to scan all the parcels. This is time that isn't paid for, but in theory they can take other work and manage their day as they like.

Facundo says, however, that supervisors punish those who fail to deliver on the day – even if the parcel is a three-to-five-day delivery – by withholding future jobs. 'One Saturday I had to go to somewhere in the afternoon and when my parcels arrived at lunchtime I delivered all the 24-hour delivery,' he explains. 'The others I delivered the next day. They were very cross and said I would have service removal if I ever did it again, and so on. So, it don't matter to them if you don't get in until 1 o'clock in the morning or you're having to knock somebody up and pissing them off at 11 o'clock at night, because somebody's monitoring you. If you want to take a day off, you need to find somebody to do your deliveries for you.'

Last summer he went to Spain to see his parents for two weeks. He gave his supervisor two months' notice that he was going, but when he came back they gave him no work at all for three weeks. 'They texted me and said, "You haven't got any rounds any more, you shouldn't have gone on holiday," ' he says, showing me the text. 'There is nothing you can do about it. You are self-employed. You work one day, they don't want you the next day, there is nowhere to go.'

According to figures from the TUC released in February 2017, the rise in so-called self-employed workers is costing the UK almost £4 billion a year in lost tax income – as the self-employed earn less than full-time employees in equivalent jobs and are more likely to need in-work benefits. The TUC, however, could be underestimating this figure. Similar numbers from the government's employment tsar, Matthew Taylor, in the same month show that self-employed workers pay at least £2,000 per year less in taxes than employees doing equivalent jobs. Given that 4.8 million, or 15 per cent, of those in work are self-employed, this means a loss of over £9 billion to the exchequer – roughly a quarter of the UK's defence budget.

But this process of casualisation and impoverishment does not just exist in warehouses and factories. I met Vicky Milroy during lambing season in the spring of 2016. With her partner Jason she was working through a flock of 1,000 ewes in a vast metal barn, divided up into small pens and larger enclosures. They'd been working this flock for four days, starting at 5.00 am every day, and had 240 ewes to go. The sheep don't belong to her. The land is owned by a woman who has a number of West Country farms, and who employs a softly spoken farm manager Vicky only knew as Rob. Vicky and Jason are freelance shepherds, for want of a better word – although she laughs when I call her that.

During shearing season she puts in twelve-hour days, trimming and sorting heavy fleeces from six in the morning. It's always been her dream to be a farmer: she's worked on farms for free, earned a 2:1 honours degree at the National Agricultural College in Cirencester and, at twenty-four, should be the future of the industry. All she wants is the chance for her and Jason to have their own county farm – a farm owned by the county that's rented out just like a council house – but, just as Chinese steel-dumping threatens to close Tata's Port Talbot steelworks, lamb, beef and wool dumping is threatening the livelihoods of British farmers.

As the world's largest consumer of wool – as well as lamb and beef – China effectively sets the global price and buys around 30 per cent of the UK's wool, according to the Wool Marketing Board. China also hosts the largest flocks of sheep in the world, and the recently booming Chinese economy's demand for textiles saw bumper wool orders and high prices for British farmers, who sold fine wool usually for over £1 per kilo during the past seven years.

China's recent economic slump, however, coupled with the strength of sterling, has seen prices plummet, with British wool selling for an average of 83p per kilo. At the same time, China has relied on its vast domestic herds for wool and lamb, forcing an oversupply of cheap New Zealand lamb originally destined for China on to the British market, drastically affecting the profitability of British farms.

'Once the demand for New Zealand lamb in China dropped in 2015 the Kiwis just turned the export boats around – literally in the middle of their voyage – and sent them to Britain,' explains Joanne Briggs at the National Sheep Association. 'That flooded our market at just the wrong time of year. The average producer running a commercial flock in a lowland situation lost £10.95 per ewe in the 2014–15 financial year. That's not sustainable.'

Figures from the National Farmers Union (NFU) released at the end of April 2016 show that the profitability of UK farming fell by a staggering 29 per cent in 2015, a loss of over £1.5 billion. This is the biggest year-on-year fall since the millennium. The NFU blamed 'a cocktail of higher production around the world, subdued demand due to slowing economies, the strength of sterling in 2015 and over twenty-four months of falling farm gate prices across the sectors'.

For Milroy, this means a drop in her already slim wages. Based near Cirencester, she has to travel the country for lambing and shearing seasons stretching over the first half of the year, then heads to Norway for an extra month's shearing. As an assistant who trims and tidies the wool, she earns roughly 28p per sheared sheep. Overall – Norwegian work included – she earns around £10,000 per year, lower than teaching assistants or apprentices. For this, she puts in over twelve hours of hard, physical work a day – up at half past four and finished by seven at night.

'Farming is going through the same decline as the pit towns and the steel towns,' she explains during a break, leaning up against a low stone wall at the edge of a large Cotswolds farm. 'It's just slower, and takes people out one at a time rather than all at once. What's pretty galling is that I work with organic lambs for a living but my wages mean I can't afford to buy organic lamb or even shop at Tesco. I have to take the cheap chicken options at cheaper supermarkets.'

Ben Briggs, editor of the *Farmers Guardian*, warns that supermarket price wars are further hitting farm income – farmers received less than £3 per kg for lamb in 2015, a poor return on a 40 kg lamb. 'Dairy farmers are even harder hit', says Briggs. 'There are farmers getting 16–17p a litre for milk compared to 35–6p a litre 18 months ago. In the mid-90s we had 35,000 dairy herds in the UK. That's fallen to 10,000 – and people are thinking it'll reach just 5,000 herds in the next ten years.'

According to figures from Savills, farmers made up 50 per cent of farmland sellers in 2016 – the highest proportion in seven years – as low commodity prices and increased debt led to early retirements, selling largely to non-farmers – including lifestyle buyers (16 per cent), investors (10 per cent) and institutional/corporate buyers (20 per cent). 'What does that do to the farming community?' asks Briggs. 'We're losing those people out of the countryside . . . the young people especially. There's lots of passionate youngsters coming through into the industry with new ideas but they need a viable industry to take those ideas forward.'

Back in the Cotswolds, Milroy is pessimistic. 'I will never earn the money to buy land round here, because it's all bought by London money,' she explains. 'Gloucestershire County Council are selling off council farms, which is our best hope, and even those would cost between £30,000 and £100,000 to equip and buy livestock. But I'm not quitting,' she insists. 'I have always wanted to do this. I've always been obsessed with agriculture. I just wish people respected farmers a little more.'

Although agency workers aren't entitled to sick pay or parental leave, or protection from unfair dismissal or redundancy, they do have their tax and National Insurance paid by their employer. The Agency Worker Regulations of 2010 give any agency worker who has been with the same firm for twelve continuous weeks the right to the same pay, holidays and pension rights as their full-time colleagues – although this is rarely enforced.

There are other emerging working arrangements, however, which increasingly blur the distinction between agency and other forms of work. A small but growing part of the workforce is paid via an umbrella company – a firm set up solely to provide payroll services. Workers in these positions may still work via an agency but, in contrast to the classic agency worker, are viewed as self-employed. They have minimal employment rights and are subject to different tax and National Insurance treatment.

According to the Resolution Foundation, some 66,000 agency workers are technically self-employed. Take Emily May, a thirty-something special needs teaching assistant. Fifteen years ago, May moved to London to study animation. After graduating, she ran animation workshops for teenagers at Fairbridge – a charity for troubled teens that's now part of the Prince's Trust. She has had permanent work ever since – everything from development tutor to trip organiser for a range of charities. In August 2015, however, the charity she was working for collapsed and she was made redundant. After signing on for a few months, she entered an agreement with her local Jobcentre to join the New Enterprise Allowance scheme – in effect an agreement to become self-employed and treat her teaching as a business. She received a weekly allowance and was assured this wouldn't affect her housing benefit, tax credits or Universal Credit.

In February 2016, Emily secured some part-time/supply special needs teacher work with Transitional Care Education Services Ltd (TCES) – a private company specialising in schooling local authority provision pupils across Essex and London, which runs three independent private schools for special educational needs (SEN) pupils. Emily was recruited by Teaching Talent – a recruitment agency specialising in supply and permanent teachers with a particular expertise in SEN pupils. Teaching Talent is wholly owned by TCES, so Emily was, in theory, employed by an agency owned by the school she was working at. Shortly after she signed up, however,

Emily found her contract was with another company entirely – a so-called umbrella company, Surrey Dock Solutions.

'The agency told me the rate was £100 a day but, after I started working, they said – you have to sign up to this umbrella company and they'll take £5 a day processing fee from your wages,' she explained. 'I didn't understand the payslips at all – there were always different National Insurance payments and the amount deducted changed all the time.'

The name of the umbrella company kept changing – one month she was employed by Surrey Dock Solutions, based at Vision House, 3 Dee Road, Richmond, TW9. The next, it was Orchid Consultancy Ltd, also based at Vision House, 3 Dee Road, Richmond, TW9. Her fellow agency employees, meanwhile, were all paid by different umbrella companies.

Orchid Consultancy's listing with Companies House shows a curious rotating director arrangement – the company was incorporated on 13 March 2016 with Pramod Patha as director and sole shareholder. On 30 March 2016, Dipen Hasmukhbai Patel was appointed as a director while Pramod Patha's appointment was terminated. In May 2016, Dipen Hasmukhbai Patel's appointment was terminated and Pramod Patha was appointed as a director. The company's single share was transferred between the two men each time.

Surrey Dock Solutions was set up by Ruairi Laughlin McCann in March 2013. In October 2014, Laughlin McCann left the company and Venkata Srikanth Polavarapu became the sole shareholder and company director. He left in April 2016, to be replaced by Dipen Hasmukhbai Patel – who also became director of Pioneer Business Consulting, also based in Suite F3, Vision House, 3 Dee Road, Richmond, TW9 . . .

a company he'd founded in 2011 and quit in 2012 to be replaced by Jayesh Javerchand Shah. Indeed, since 2011 Dipen Hasmukhbai Patel has been director of fifty-nine companies – for forty-three of these he was appointed director on 30 March 2016 and resigned on 6 May 2016.

Vision House, 3 Dee Road, Richmond, TW9 is a bland, flat-fronted office building opposite a housing estate in Richmond. It's officially the office of Financial Partnership LLP, a firm of accountants – founded by Dipen Hasmukhbai Patel and Jayesh Javerchand Shah in December 2014, shortly after Jayesh Javerchand Shah dissolved Financial Partners London Ltd. Dipen Hasmukhbai Patel resigned as a director on 11 April 2016.

In the past five years, Suite F1–F3 of Vision House has been home to almost sixty different companies – many now dissolved – including Dial A Meal, O3 Technology Solutions, Harley Street Cosmetic Doctors Ltd, Greenspace Homes, Car Minds UK, Ryan Surveillance Services and Bude Interiors and Consulting. These companies are part of Financial Partnership LLP's payroll services offer – paper companies that hold employees' contracts, putting them in a state of permanent rights-free limbo and leeching additional money from their already low wages.

'There's layers now between everything where there didn't used to be,' Emily said in a quiet, tired voice. 'When you order a takeaway, a different company will deliver it to you. When you go and work for someone people are inserting themselves in-between everything in order to make money out of every step. I suppose it's quite clever really – but who benefits from it? I was very concerned when I worked at TCES about the way things are done – and about the whole business of having temps working with children in special education needs. I was put in rooms with children with really complex behavioural difficulties and not given any background. Then they start kicking the wall and I'd not have adequate information to handle that.'

Emily showed me some of her payslips – one week her total income was £500, but the Surrey Dock/Orchid rotating umbrella company paid Emily's employer National Insurance contributions out of her salary and took a £20 processing fee for doing so, lopping £50.85 off her income. The following week the same payments came to £51.17. The company deducted PAYE (Pay As You Earn) tax and employee National Insurance – one week that came to £60.55, the next it was £61.22. They also retained £3 – alternately described on her payslip as student loan repayments or simply 'retained by company' – making her total payment roughly £385, depending on fluctuating deductions. With thirty-nine weeks of term time in the UK, this meant she could earn just over £15,000 in a year.

Her rent is £700 per month – for a damp one-bedroom flat shared with her husband and three-year-old son. While she was working, her son attended a local nursery, which cost £150 per week. The almost £8,000 needed for childcare and the £8,400 she needed for rent would have effectively wiped out her salary without support from housing benefit and child tax credit. Emily's husband works in the music industry on extremely short-term contracts. Although between them the couple were earning around £20,000, the cost of rent, childcare, food and bills proved overwhelming.

The only benefit Emily could see in the arrangement was that – as she was self-employed – she could stay on the NEA scheme. 'I was working more hours than I had originally put in my business plan – but I didn't call them until June because I just thought it'll be alright,' she explained. 'They told me that your income and hours were totted up at the end of the tax year.'

In July, however, when she tried to renew her child tax credits – paid to low-income working parents to help with childcare costs – she submitted her earnings and a week later was told she'd been overpaid, that the work she'd done between February and June meant she wasn't eligible for anything – in fact, she owed them money so she wouldn't receive any child tax credit until she'd paid it off.

Emily appealed – when she was working part-time at the charity she'd been on £20,000 per year and had received tax credits towards childcare. If she'd earned £385 per week for fifty-two weeks, she'd have been on £20,000. She asked if she could reduce the amount taken from her tax credits every month – she didn't see how she could afford her son's nursery fees. She was told they couldn't respond to anything until ten weeks after the date she'd submitted her renewal. She couldn't call until 10 October.

She spent the summer working for a friend but started drifting into debt with the nursery – she currently owes them £700. 'I just thought when I gave the new employment figure it would all recalibrate and that would sort it out, but because I'd put in the renewal they couldn't talk to me to tell me what the problem was,' she explained, in a soft, plaintive voice. 'I don't know what the problem is and no one will talk to me on the phone.'

She was talking to a group of friends about her plight – 'They were all smart, liberal, *Guardian*-reading people,' she recalls. 'I described my situation and they just couldn't grasp what it's like to go to the Jobcentre and be spoken to like you're trash or have your pay packet snipped away at by odd companies you've never heard of. Only one woman got it — she'd been made redundant around the same time. She said, Emily — people don't realise they're only a few steps from the same situation that we're in. They're just one or two steps from being unemployed, being on housing benefit and being close to trouble.'

6

Squalor

The problem of Rent:

Rent has three characteristics differentiating it from other forms of expenditure:

(i) Rent varies markedly from one part of the country to another,

(ii) Rent varies markedly as between different families of the same size in the same part of the country,

(iii) Expenditure on rent cannot be reduced during a temporary interruption of earning as that on clothing, fuel or light can.

Sir William Beveridge, *Social Insurance and Allied Services Report*

Beth is nine years old and she's had to move house three times in her short life. Recently her family were evicted when their shorthold tenancy came to an end and they all had to move into a much smaller place. She now has a tiny bedroom – so small that all her things are stored in a box as there's only room for the bed. She had to leave her hamster behind – she's not sure what happened to it – because no pets are allowed in her current house.

She doesn't like the neighbourhood she's moved into. Neighbours on both sides drink and take drugs and she doesn't feel safe. She keeps her bedroom windows closed no matter how hot her room is in summer – she's constantly anxious that someone will break in. Moving this far meant leaving her old primary school and trying to make friends at her new one, and everything makes her uneasy. 'What if, one day, where my mum's so much in debt that we get evicted and then I come back from school and all our stuff is outside?' she frets. 'And then we've got nowhere to live. What if that happens?'

In 2015, the Children's Society began a longitudinal study of children in poverty. They found sixty families with kids receiving free school meals and interviewed them regularly, planning to stay in touch for seven years to see how the children were affected by their situation. Researchers hadn't expected to discuss transience, but it came up time and time again in the interviews: families having to constantly move home, children never feeling like they have a stable home, living an almost nomadic lifestyle that has terrible outcomes for everything from health to education.

It's hugely stressful for children. 'I'm worried about moving . . . because first, if you can't find a house you might have to go to the homeless place and then those houses are really little,' one ten-year-old boy told the team. 'I'm just thinking why couldn't they just let us live in one place instead of keep moving around,' an eleven-year-old boy said. 'We stay there for like two, three, four months then we have to start packing again – then we have to leave, unpack . . . it just keeps going like that.' And many of these houses were barely fit to live in. They are damp and cramped. 'Some of the houses had a problem, like ... there were rats,' a ten-year-old boy told the researchers. 'Then when we moved to the next place there was just dead rats, they were just dead and no one took them out.'

According to the housing charity Shelter, in October 2016 over 40 per cent of rental homes in the UK fail to live up to minimum standards of acceptable conditions, with reports of persistent pests, damp and safety hazards. More than 400,000 working households live in private rented homes with category 1 hazards as defined by the English Housing Survey. These include severe health threats from damp and mould, pests, electrical installations, excess cold and dangerous levels of carbon monoxide, lead and other chemicals, including asbestos. Private rental accommodation was the worst. Landlords often covered up or painted over faults when showing new tenants round. One in three people surveyed said the problem was there when they moved in but they weren't told about it. And few private renters wanted to complain. One in ten were worried they'd be kicked out if they made a fuss.

Beveridge was horrified by housing conditions in pre-war Britain, which he identified as a source of poverty and squalor. His report argued for an ambitious council house-building programme with strong rent controls, and proposed a 'living tapestry of the mixed community', offering a mix of social housing and market housing in which 'the doctor, the grocer, the butcher and the farm labourer all lived in the same street'. By 1948, just three years after the end of the war, some 227,000 houses were built. Since then, things have changed. In 2015 – with the population 70 per cent larger – 142,890 homes were completed.

Post-war council housing initially attracted young couples and working-class families, and in 1978 over 30 per cent of all homes were social rented. Despite Beveridge's best intentions, there were inadvertent social problems created by insensitive councils rehousing families during the post-war slum clearances. Neighbours were rarely moved in next door to each other, often living miles apart on new-build estates. Tower blocks built as an experiment in utopian living turned into sink estates, partly through poor design and partly through the failure to move neighbours together to help recreate communities.

In the 1980s, the Conservative government's flagship right-to-buy policy, which allowed council tenants to buy their homes at a heavily discounted rate, marked the single greatest transfer of capital to the working class the UK has ever seen. In the first three decades of the scheme, over 2 million council properties were sold and councils were forbidden to build replacement homes.

With more affluent tenants buying their council homes and often selling them on to private landlords, the social profile of council and affordable housing tenants drifted, destroying Beveridge's 'living tapestry of the mixed community'. Today, over 30 per cent of ex-council homes in London are private rental properties. That this social cleansing goes unremarked may have something to do with shows like Channel 4's documentary series *Benefits Street*, which have helped secure the image of workless social housing and housing benefit claimants as part of a culture of poverty.

Interestingly, the myth of generations of workless families is almost entirely unfounded. In 2012, the Joseph

Rowntree Foundation undertook intensive fieldwork in deprived neighbourhoods of Glasgow and Middlesbrough, and was unable to locate a single family with three generations who had never worked. All families would have preferred to be in work rather than on benefits, workless parents were unanimous in not wanting their children to end up in the same situation and working-age children were keen to avoid worklessness.

In the same year, Lindsey Macmillan and Paul Gregg analysed data from the Labour Force Survey, the National Child Development Study and the British Household Panel Survey and found just 0.3 per cent – or 15,000 households – where two generations haven't worked. Tracking fathers and sons, they found that under 2 per cent of sons have never worked by age twenty-three and under 1 per cent have never worked by age twenty-nine.

All the same, successive UK governments have seen people on low incomes as something to be tidied away out of sight. In 1951, in response to a Labour government initiative, pit villages in County Durham's coal mining area were classified as A, B, C or D settlements. Category D settlements were to be wound down – with no new building, and existing property being acquired and demolished and the population relocated. In the face of fierce local resistance, only three villages were completely destroyed. Elsewhere many communities lost streets, houses, shops and pubs.

The 1980s Conservative government also discussed running down poorer areas – in this case, troublesome industrial cities, according to cabinet papers released in 2011. Following the 1981 riots that swept through urban areas, the environment secretary, Michael Heseltine, pleaded for £100 million to be invested in Merseyside to arrest urban decay and reduce unemployment. In response, Geoffrey Howe, then chancellor, and Keith Joseph, then industry secretary, argued for 'managed decline' and 'managed rundown' respectively.

This policy re-emerged twenty years later, when the New Labour government launched the Housing Market Renewal Pathfinder Programme – launched in 2003 with a budget of £2.2 billion. It planned to tackle housing problems in northern cities by bulldozing 250,000 houses and encouraging 1 million people to move south into new houses built near airports, where they'd help secure London as a financial hub for Europe in the face of a sudden challenge from Frankfurt. Birmingham, Staffordshire, Manchester, Merseyside, South Yorkshire, Hull, Newcastle, Oldham and East Lancashire all saw streets forcibly emptied. Residents who resisted were left alone in their homes surrounded by empty, boarded-up houses and bull-dozed neighbourhoods, cleared in some cases to prepare for new, private homes. 'What was particularly frustrating about the way they did things in Stoke is that they created an affordable housing problem by knocking down the area's affordable housing,' says Stoke-based housing and regeneration consultant Dave Proudlove. 'It's one of the reasons why many people in town are sick to the back teeth of regeneration – what is being done in places really gives regeneration a bad name.'

Today there's a vague general agreement that we 'need to build more houses'. There's no doubt we've got plenty of room to do so – 6.8 per cent of the UK is classified as urban, that is, covered by buildings and roads. Within that 6.8 per cent just over half – 54 per cent – is green space, made up of parks, allotments and sports fields. Domestic gardens account for another 18 per cent of urban land, with rivers, canals, lakes and reservoirs taking up 6.6 per cent. This means the proportion of the UK that is built on is 2.27 per cent, and the proportion occupied by domestic dwellings – houses and flats – is just 1.1 per cent. In 2013, Colin Wiles, an independent housing consultant and former housing association chief executive, worked through the uses of land in the UK for the *Inside Housing* blog and calculated that golf courses in the UK also covered 1.1 per cent.

So, demolishing homes makes little or no sense and just makes people feel ignored and angry. In Stoke, hundreds of homes were bulldozed and, by the time of the general election in 2010, few homes had been built to replace them. The Pathfinder programme was clearly flawed, but the incoming coalition government's response – to stop the programme dead four years early – was equally problematic. In street after street, houses had already been emptied and boarded up for bulldozing. What have been left behind are dead, shuttered streets and derelict ground. In Middleport, in Stoke, this means 250 missing homes left to rot.

It's hard to describe how barren and lifeless these streets feel. The steel shutters look so wrong, like a deadly growth on a much-loved tree. Walking along Newport Lane in Middleport, fully half the street has been gutted – walking south from the junction with Lucas Street, the houses on the right have been shuttered for so long that the metal is starting to rust away and a patch of derelict ground on the left is closed off by a tatty, graffiti-covered solid wooden fence.

These destructive ideas continue to flourish. As recently as 2015, the architect who designed the Welsh Millennium Centre, Jonathan Adams, argued that the Welsh Valleys were gradually depopulating, with younger people drifting south, and that this process should be encouraged. He suggested demolishing unattractive houses to reduce town sizes and sprucing the older buildings up to make them more attractive to tourists. In effect, this meant moving swathes of the population to Cardiff and making the Valleys into a national park.

These ideas almost always fail, leaving low-income families worse off than before. In the long term even the right-to-buy policy and its target of a 'property-owning democracy' failed. The ban on councils building new houses has contributed to the shortage of homes that's slowly throttling the country. Across London, in the six years to the end of 2016 the number of new homes built accounts for just 41.8 per cent of the number of new households formed in the same period, according to GMB analysis of housing and planning data from the Department for Communities and Local Government.

In February 2017, Oxford Economics analysed official figures and found there were more than 1 million empty homes in the UK – mostly second homes or vacant properties. Meanwhile, fewer people own their home either outright or with a mortgage than at any time since 1986.

Nationally, the number of working households privately renting has almost doubled from 2.5 to 4.8 million over the past ten years, according to figures from the Department for Communities and Local Government, while the number of families with children that are privately renting has tripled, to 1.5 million.

This has a direct impact on poverty levels, education, employment prospects and stable communities. More than

70 per cent of private renters in the poorest fifth spend at least a third of their income on housing, compared with under 50 per cent in the social rented sector and 28 per cent for those who own their own homes

The private rented sector is much less stable than social renting or owner occupancy. According to the Department for Communities and Local Government's English Housing Survey, 40 per cent of tenancy agreements are for six months or less. Thirty per cent of renters in the private sector have been in their current accommodation for a year or less; for social housing renters, that figure is below 10 per cent. Private tenants have very weak security of tenure – there are three main kinds of fixed-term contracts: twelve months, six months and rolling four-week contracts. Outside of the fixed term, landlords can evict tenants for any reason or no reason.

'We've found people who have fallen behind on their rent a couple of times over twelve months, paying late, losing their tenancy because landlords don't want the hassle,' says John Bibby, a policy officer at housing charity Shelter. 'Even if you're trying your hardest to make ends meet you stand to lose your home. If you complain to the landlord, there is a risk that they chuck you out. Anything you might have done to irritate a landlord you might lose your home. Ten years ago, only one in ten families were in private rented accommodation – now its one in four. It's unacceptable that these people have no guarantee of their home beyond twelve months.'

Some 58,000 households were accepted as homeless in 2015–16, an increase of almost 50 per cent over the past five years, with the most common cause being the end of a short-hold tenancy or rent arrears. Government data show that, in the third quarter of 2016, 74,630 households, including 117,520 children, were living in temporary accommodation – from women's refuges through bed and breakfasts to temporary housing associations or council sites. In December 2016, a report from the Institute for Public Policy Research found that the majority of the 6,680 families placed in emergency short-term bed and breakfast accommodation had been there for at least twelve months. One had lived in temporary accommodation for thirty-six years. When Shelter collated figures on rough sleepers, temporary accommodation, hostels and people waiting to be housed, the housing charity estimates that 254,514 people were homeless at the end of 2016, describing this number as 'a robust lower-end estimate'.

In January 2016 I met eight-year-old Kelly Louise, from Luton, who had just moved into temporary accommodation because the landlord was selling the house her family were renting. 'We had to wait until the council found us a place to live,' she explains, choosing her words carefully. 'I was really nervous and my mum was so stressed – it made me feel helpless. When we moved to a hostel, the stress didn't go away. Everyone is unhappy in that place. My family is all in one room. We're lucky – we have a bathroom but the sink was hanging off the wall. Other families don't even have a bathroom. I don't want my mum to get stressed so every time I feel sad or worried, I pinch myself – pinching my feelings and keeping them inside.'

And there's further social drifting – a more delicate word than cleansing – underway thanks to recent changes to housing benefit. The Local Housing Allowance (LHA) sets the level of housing benefit available for tenants in the private rented sector. In place since 2008, a set amount is paid, according to the average price for homes in the area, regardless of the actual rent. At launch, the maximum rent considered acceptable was the fiftieth percentile of local rents – of one hundred houses in a local area people could get housing benefit to cover the rents of the cheapest fifty homes.

In 2010 the coalition government reduced this to the cheapest 30 per cent of homes, and then froze housing benefit at that level. The following year it was raised by the consumer prices index measure of inflation, rather than local rents, followed by two years of 1 per cent rises before being frozen again until the end of the decade. 'The freeze means the LHA is not being increased at the same levels as rents,' explains Bibby. 'So now the amount paid is not even enough to cover rent at the thirtieth percentile. We're seeing gaps open up between the amount of benefit people receive and the amount of rent they have to pay.'

LHA rates for the whole of the UK can be found online (at lha.direct.voa.gov.uk). The maximum benefit for a room in shared accommodation in Manchester, for instance, is £291 per month; the maximum for a one-bedroom flat is £441 per month; for a two-bedroom flat it's £519 per month; and for three bedrooms it's £577 per month.

Once a year, the Valuation Office Agency publishes rent statistics in the private rental markets – breaking down average and lowest available rents by area. The easiest way to find that is to search online for 'rent statistics voa'. November 2016 figures show that the lowest rent for shared accommodation in Manchester is £325 per month; for a one-bedroom flat it's £516 per month; two bedrooms is £585 per month; and three bedrooms is £630 per month.

A significant number of those receiving housing benefit in the private rented sector are in work, and the government expects them to increase their income with more hours, or better work, to cover the rental gap. Often that's not possible: there may not be more hours or a better job available. For parents, the increased childcare costs can make working more hours unaffordable. And for groups like pensioners or people on Employment and Support Allowance, there's nowhere to find the extra except from the money you have for food and clothes. Shelter research in September 2016 found nearly half of working families – roughly 3.7 million of them – cutting back on essential food and clothing to pay the rent. Around one in five cut back on children's clothing, while around one in ten had skipped meals.

And the arrival of Universal Credit is making everything much harder. The benefit comes as a single monthly payment – leaving the claimant to pay rent, food, bills, clothes and transport from the lump sum. It has broken the link between housing benefit and the rent that people actually pay, dismissing at a stroke Beveridge's key problem. 'With the present variety of rents, it is not possible to fix any uniform rate of insurance benefit as meeting subsistence requirements with any accuracy,' he wrote.

In August 2016, 324,058 people were claiming Universal Credit, a figure that's rising by around 17,000 each month. In June 2016, the National Federation of Arm's Length Management Organisations (NFA) and the Association of Retained Council Housing found 79 per cent of tenants on Universal Credit in council housing were in rent arrears, compared to 31 per cent of other tenants. In October 2016, housing association data-cruncher HouseMark reported that the average rent arrears debt of a Universal Credit claimant was £618 per property, compared to average non-Universal Credit arrears of £131. With average social rents around £96 per week, this Universal Credit debt is roughly six to seven weeks' rent.

Many are forced to move house. Between 2010 and 2016, one-third of housing benefit claimants in private rented accommodation in London moved out of their borough. Professor Nick Bailey, from the University of Glasgow's urban studies division, calls it the 'suburbanisation of poverty'. 'British cities have seen thousands of people on lower incomes move from the inner city to the outer boroughs in the last twelve years thanks to a loss of social housing and cuts to welfare benefits,' he explains. 'If you took an area that size and cleared it there would be political uproar. But what is happening is so fragmented that it is almost passing without comment.'

In Peckham, South London, for instance, I met Emily as she prepared to leave the city and take her son to live with her grandmother in Norfolk. Although she worked part-time, the low pay and falling housing benefit meant their one-bedroom flat with rising, penetrating damp was too expensive. 'The walls are wet to the touch,' she explained. 'I fixed some of the problems myself by repainting the wall and the outside windows but there's some wet always coming through. There's no soundproofing and we've got neighbours upstairs and they keep my son awake. I was looking at the costs of flats in the area for anywhere in London and there's nothing that we could afford. Nothing. There was one night when my son didn't sleep at all. I was awake from five in the morning looking at the damp and then wandered into my kitchen and saw a mouse – which is not the end of the world but it felt like – if I don't do something radical this is only going to get worse.'

In December 2016, Shelter combined government statistics, FOI requests and published homelessness data to calculate the total number of homeless people in the UK – almost 255,000. Most of these are in some sort of temporary accommodation. The latest available figures from rough-sleeper charity Crisis suggests that there are around 4,134 rough sleepers in England, 1,787 in Scotland and 240 in Wales. However, outreach services working with the Combined Homelessness and Information Network reported 8,096 specific individuals sleeping rough in London at some point during 2015–16, up 7 per cent on 2014–15.

In Leicester, rough sleepers tend to congregate along the canal. Some squat in old warehouses. Others pitch a tent or construct makeshift wooden shelters in a kind of shanty town. The city has a GP practice and social enterprise running the city's homeless healthcare – called Inclusion, it was founded by CEO Anna Hiley and executive director Jane Gray when their homeless healthcare contract was put up for tender in 2011. 'I was the GP and Jane was the nurse,' Hiley explains when we meet in her office on a wet, wintry day. 'They were going to put us out to tender on the open market and we were determined that we would not let our service be taken over by a for-profit organisation.'

She's seen 'an awful lot of single males who have had a really nice family and then lost everything – they're in their forties and fifties', she explains, staring at her hands. 'Some of them weren't that much older than me and I'm in my forties. And after seeing how, I look at my husband and think what would happen if we'd split up. How would his path be? And a lot of these people aren't visible. They may sleep on a friend's sofa, but that can't be done long-term. We've spoken to people living in garden sheds or garages.'

Women, she explains, tend to have been exploited, working on the streets, become substance abusers, victims of domestic violence or have been trafficked. 'So they tend to be using drugs or alcohol or both – only a quarter of our patients are females but they tend to be in a more desperate state.' She gives a small, tight smile.

Quite often, she believes, depression has had a part to play. 'Perhaps something's happened within the family or their relationship is not working very well or they've lost their job and they've taken to alcohol,' she nods. 'That tends to be the scenario. Sometimes children are involved and the man leaves so that their partner and the children have somewhere secure. Perhaps they find themselves somewhere like a bedsit, and they drink and they're not attending work properly or they're late. They don't want to go and ask for help out of pride so things keep getting worse and worse.'

That afternoon I visited the city's wet centre: a day hostel that allows homeless people to walk in drunk or on drugs. As I arrived, staff were struggling to help a man suffering from the violent hallucinations and sweeping emotional changes brought on by the synthetic cannabinoid Black Mamba. He was howling, his body shaking and his eyes blank. 'It's cheap and it's strong,' Hiley explains. 'It's sweeping through prisons and the homeless and the effects are brutal. People are using it to find oblivion.'

Back in the main building – a walk-in and advice centre in a spruced up old school – I met Jas Singh, one of Inclusion's regulars and a local lad. He's fresh-faced and handsome – he looks a little like Stone Roses singer Ian Brown, right down to his jagged mop-top hair – but he totters into the room on crutches with his foot strapped up in a large webbing-and-plastic sandal. Singh studied art at St Martins and graduated in 2012, moving to Kingston upon Thames where a friend secured him a protection-by-occupation residency in a large empty house. He was on the verge of the next stage in his life – interning with an art dealer on Pimlico Road. 'It was unpaid but I'd get fed and into all the art exhibitions for free, and some champagne parties,' he grins. 'I started to meet a few people – like Terry O'Neill, the photographer, and I was starting to put my own work together . . . mainly sound installations.'

And then, running up the stairs at the art dealer's house in 2014, Jas slipped and whacked his leg on the corner of a stair and damaged his peroneal nerve, which provides feeling to the front and side of the legs and the top of the feet. A damaged peroneal nerve causes a condition known as foot drop, where the muscles that hold the foot in place stop working and the patient's foot effectively dangles uselessly at the end of their leg. He couldn't walk without crutches and couldn't keep working with the art dealer. When the house he was legally squatting finally got sold, he was out – just as his dad phoned to tell him his mum was ill, asking him to come back to Leicester to help out.

'So I came back for a while,' he explains. 'I was here for about six months when, ironically, I was giving a homeless person a few bits of change and got mugged, whacked on the back of my head – I was knocked out, unconscious for a while. I'm still not clear on everything that happened after that. Apparently I discharged myself and went back to my family with my head still bleeding. We had a huge row – I can't remember what about . . . I was drinking at that time though I'm sober now. But the atmosphere was tense.'

Mood swings, anger and tears are textbook behaviours after a head injury – although Singh blames long-running family tension for the rows that simmered at home. After two weeks, he slipped on the stairs again and fractured the same foot. An ambulance took him to hospital and his last words to his dad were – 'I'll call you as soon as I'm done.'

After his foot was treated, he stood outside Leicester General Hospital waiting for his dad when he got a tap on his shoulder. 'It's two police and it's like – are you Mr Singh?' he recalls, shaking his head. 'I'm thinking – why are the police asking if I'm Mr Singh?' He pauses for a moment and looks away, then back. 'And I get arrested by the police – they say they've a restraining order because of my aggression at my dad's house . . . and I'm kind of baffled because I just had a conversation with my dad and I thought he was coming to pick me up . . . but it turns out suddenly I'm homeless.'

After a night at Euston Police Station, a squad car dropped him off at the Dawn Centre, Leicester's last remaining homeless hostel – the council has closed three other hostels in the past few years, offering supported accommodation instead but effectively reducing the number of beds available to rough sleepers. Still a little dazed – and with a few belongings in a plastic bag – he was hoping to get to a bed early to rest and recover a little. But the Dawn Centre was full and the hotels he could walk to only had rooms for £70 a night, so he went to an off-licence, bought a few cans of Kronenberg and slipped into a hotel car park where he lay down behind a parked van – 'and drank and drank and tried to sleep,' he shivers. 'It was February and I was freezing so I thought I'd knock myself out with alcohol. But when you try and sleep outside, you think you've slept and then you look at your phone and it's been three minutes.'

He was so exhausted and dirty he thought he couldn't do another night like that so he booked in to the hotel using his bank card to guarantee the room. He had a shower and got his head down for a couple of hours. When he woke, his phone battery was running low, he had no money and everything he owned was at his parents' house. He walked on his crutches over to Leicester City Council housing office, where they said he wasn't eligible for help as his parents' house, his last address, stands just outside the city limits in Leicestershire.

He managed to get an appointment with Oadby and Wigston Borough Council on the same day, got to the bus stop and realised he just had a few coppers and a little bit of change. He showed the bus driver all he had, and told him where he was going. The driver just took a few of the coppers and let him on, which still brings tears to his eyes when he tells the story. At Oadby and Wigston, a housing officer called Heidi hunted out a bed at the Action Homeless hostel, run by a local charity in the city centre. She lent him £3 to get the bus, he made it to Victoria Park and was given a bed on the first floor of a brick townhouse. He made friends sharing tobacco and Rizla – 'it was like school or a prison', he says. 'I hadn't got my own cup so they wouldn't give me tea. People were kicking off over dinner and I almost wished I was outside again, instead of having to climb the stairs to get to my room with the noise of someone kicking off every half an hour.'

They moved him around a couple of times. First into shared accommodation and finally into a single room in a quieter house. The bureaucracy of the homeless system proved endlessly baffling. One advisor told him he wasn't entitled to housing in Leicester because his family lived outside, but if he filled out a form saying he was estranged from his family that would see him clear. So he did that and got a letter back saying he wasn't eligible because he had no local connections. He'd have to wait in limbo for two years before he became a resident of Leicester.

'It's crazy,' he explains. 'There's housing I can get for £385 per month, and the council is paying my hostel over £780 for a single room with a shared kitchen. On top of that, I pay the hostel £104 a month, so they're clearing £900 per month. Every now and then, someone says they may force me back to London, because I have connections there. But how am I going to get on a waiting list in Kingston upon Thames of all places?'

He was sleeping badly, and hugely sensitive to noise and light, which eventually drove him to Inclusion looking for something to help. There he met a Dr Maxwell, who talked to him for half an hour and was shocked that he'd not been treated for his head injury. She helped sort out some medication, got the in-house physiotherapist to look at his leg and wrote a few letters to Action Homeless explaining his illness and asking that he be moved to a less noisy building. She also connected him with Headway, a charity dealing with people with head injuries, who secured him an assessment for the Employment and Support Allowance – the benefit paid to disabled people. Initially the interview was scheduled in Nottingham. 'I told them I had problems with my leg and I suffer from anxiety,' he shrugs. 'Does it make sense to send me to Nottingham? And because I'm band four – as in, I'm not drinking or doing drugs – I'm a long way down the list for any better accommodation. So if I get myself an addiction I'd get housed. I'd be better off if I started taking drugs.'

The days pass slowly, he says – he's got a scrapbook and tries doodling and sketching in it. He's got a few ideas but they don't quite come out right. And he's started to help out at a homeless charity Open Hands.

'They're all charities aren't they? It's funny that. The thing is – it can happen to anyone. I see people buying all these lottery tickets and it's like – you've got more chance of being homeless than winning the lottery you know? I was working towards an okay life before – interning and organising exhibitions in Pimlico and Chelsea. Now everything's stripped away. Some people do help out – but most people think I don't look homeless enough.'

7

Unconnected

Social security must be achieved by co-operation between the State and the individual. The State — in organising security — should not stifle incentive, opportunity or responsibility.

Sir William Beveridge, *Social Insurance and Allied Services Report*

In 2015, Nick East was fined by the government for not having broadband. He'd been unemployed for eighteen months after losing his job as a kitchen porter in a country pub. His ageing motorbike finally collapsed and he didn't have the money to replace her. The bus was irregular and dropped off some way from the village, so he was late one time too many. When he signed on the Jobcentre told him to apply for a minimum of twenty-four jobs per week on Universal Jobmatch – the government's digital replacement for the old Jobcentre notice board.

Universal Jobmatch seems like a smart response to the digital age. The Jobcentre can monitor all online activity to make sure people are actively hunting for work. If they don't meet their targets – twenty-four jobs in Nick's case – people get sanctioned, losing all benefits for anything from four weeks to three years. But applying for twenty-four jobs on Universal Jobmatch is a complex and time-consuming business at best. You can't upload your CV for most roles and have to type each line of the form out, adding in the same work record time after time. If you don't have broadband, it's far worse.

Nick had to travel to Newcastle's city centre library from his flat in Newbiggin – a good thirty minutes away, with one bus every half an hour and a return ticket costing £3.90. Nick was travelling in three days a week, costing him £12 taken from his £52 Jobseeker's Allowance benefit, leaving him just over £5 per day before paying for food, bills or clothes. Newcastle library allows members two hours free computer use in its well-appointed fourth-floor computer room that hosts forty computers and a handful of iMacs, and is almost always packed. In a high-tech version of the old casual labour scrums outside the local docks, he'd scramble for a free screen when the library doors opened. 'You have to get there very early', the twenty-four-year-old explains, 'or all the screens will be gone and you have to hang around. And you can't afford a city centre coffee so you just walk about the streets.'

Each job took a minimum of half an hour to apply for, up to an hour if there were added questionnaires on skills – meaning anything from ten to twenty-four hours per week online. If he reached the end of his two-hour session, Universal Jobmatch wouldn't allow him to save his application, meaning if he hadn't finished he'd have to start all over again when a new computer came free.

Four months ago, he failed to hit twenty-four applications and received an official warning: 'There just weren't the jobs. I was down for bar work, factory work and general labouring but there weren't any jobs. Three months ago, I couldn't make it in to the library four times – I had no money – so I didn't hit twenty-four again and they sanctioned me. Four weeks with no money – they took my JSA [Jobseeker's Allowance], my housing benefit and council tax benefit. I had nothing.'

It's not like he doesn't keep trying, he explains earnestly. When he was a kid, he wanted to work on the oil rigs. On Sunday evenings he sometimes saw the riggers, laden down with kit, on the way to Newcastle Airport for the Aberdeen flight. His uncle worked the rigs for forty years and made a good living. He'd still love the job – but before he can apply he has to pay for a two-day Client Contractor National Safety Group Site Safety Passport course and an offshore survival and fire-fighting course, which comes in at around £2,000. 'I asked the Jobcentre to help with the course, but they said no, and they refused to help for a fork-lift truck training course.' He shrugs helplessly. 'So I can't apply for skilled jobs and there aren't enough general jobs for me and the other forty people online at the library. Maybe they're all going to people who can log in any time from their sofa.'

Over in Wigan, Lisa Wright, a former factory worker who was on Jobseeker's Allowance for three years after the food processing plant she worked for closed, is doing a six-month community work programme in the kitchen at Sunshine House, a community centre in Scholes just two minutes' walk from Darlington Street, which once housed the infamous tripe shop George Orwell stayed in while writing *The Road to Wigan Pier*. Alongside her mandated thirty hours community service, Lisa has to put in ten hours a week on Universal Jobmatch.

'I can only get to a computer in Wigan library on Thursday evenings, Fridays and Saturday mornings,' she explains. 'There's sometimes a queue so you can hang around for up to an hour. That's the only time I can check my e-mails, which means if I get sent a reply to a job application on Monday I don't see it for days.'

If you don't have your own computer, she points out, you're on a tight timeframe. 'I like to do an application and then go back to it and make sure it's good – but when you're using a shared computer someone else is always waiting,' she explains. 'You're cutting and pasting things from another application. It feels like you're constantly doing things wrong and struggling just to keep up.' She met a kid last week doing 200 hours, community service for robbing a shop. 'I'm doing 780 hours, community service and my only crime is being unemployed,' she sighs.

One of the most deprived areas in the country is Speke, Liverpool. It was designed as a post-war garden suburb built around a cluster of factories, but the factories closed in the late 1970s and early 1980s. 'Around 85 per cent of our clients don't even have e-mail addresses,' says Bob Wilson at Speke Citizens Advice Bureau. 'And we've got clients showing up at the door hoping to see an adviser who haven't been able to call ahead because their phone has run out of credit all the time. We have clients coming in to use the phone because they've got no phone credit and a call to the DWP to appeal a sanction takes anything from forty minutes to an hour – on 0800 numbers, which cost 40p per minute from a mobile phone.'

According to Ofcom figures for 2016, roughly 20 per cent of UK adults – one-fifth of the country – don't have broadband access at home (see figure below). This has remained unchanged since 2015 despite the government's digital inclusion strategy, announced in 2014 with the aim of reducing the number of people offline by 25 per cent every two years. By 2020, according to then minister for the cabinet office Francis Maude, the UK will have reduced the number of people who lack basic digital skills or access to around 4.7 million – less than 10 per cent of the adult population. Three years down the line, with numbers barely changing, that seems unlikely.

Internet reach (2016)

% of all respondents	% All UK 16+	Age 16-24	25-34	35-44	45-54	55-64	65-74	55+	65+	75+	Gender Male	Female	Socio-economic/income ABC1	C2DE	DE	Unemployed	Low income	Low income/children in home	Location/nation Urban	Rural	England	Scotland	Wales	N. Ireland	BAME	Disability
Base	3737	519	604	602	570	578	481	1442	864	383	1790	1947	1919	1813	1022	251	559	155	2711	1026	2339	502	489	507	222	744
Ever use the internet anywhere?	87	97	97	96	93	87	72	71	58	42	87	87	93	81	77	87	68	92	87	88	87	87	86	83	94	64
% change since 2015	+1																					+7			n/a	n/a
Broadband take-up	81	86	81	88	91	83	74	70	59	43	81	80	87	73	65	67	55	73	80	85	81	79	79	78	83	60
% change since 2015	+1			+4													+4							+6	n/a	n/a
Use mobile phone to go online	66	89	89	84	70	50	31	33	19	6	64	67	70	60	57	65	46	81	66	61	66	63	61	69	77	36
% change since 2015	+5				+11		+8					+6		+7	+8			+17	+4		+5			+9	n/a	n/a
Use internet at work/college	40	64	54	56	45	27	6	14	4	3	43	38	52	27	17	8	14	22	41	35	40	44	35	39	48	14
% change since 2015	0																								n/a	n/a
Use internet at a library	7	15	8	7	4	3	4	4	3	2	7	6	8	5	6	8	7	7	7	3	7	4	5	7	10	3
% change since 2015	+1																								n/a	n/a

Note: Empty cells indicate a zero percentage.

Breaking the Ofcom figures down by social class we find that on average, 93 per cent of ABC1s use the internet regularly on any device, compared to 81 per cent of C2DEs, 77 per cent of DEs and 68 per cent of low-income households – although this final number rises to 92 per cent for low-income houses with children. Broadband take-up follows a similar pattern: 87 per cent for ABC1s, 73 per cent for C2DEs, 65 per cent for DEs and 55 per cent for low-income households, rising to 73 per cent for low-income households with kids. Using a mobile to go online maps the same trajectory: ABC1 70 per cent, C2DE 60 per cent, DE 57 per cent, low-income 46 per cent and low-income with kids 81 per cent.

In other words, those on low incomes are not just materially deprived, they are digitally deprived, at a time when the government is moving more and more services online and the country is racing towards an increasingly digitised political sphere where online petitions and Twitter storms can influence government policy. It's harder for low-income families to take part in debates, read online newspapers, research essays for school or college and even to lobby their MPs.

There's a digital democracy deficit looming, according to Mike Harris, CEO of policy and public affairs consultancy 89Up. 'We're building a digital toolkit to let charities and citizens get in touch with their prospective parliamentary candidates and ask them key questions,' he explains. 'The internet is cutting the cost for each individual to lobby the people who hope to represent them – but only because people are buying their own computers and smartphones and paying for broadband. We're asking people to subsidise this in other words. If 20 per cent of the country can't take part in this, they can't be part of the conversation.'

'The primary reason people don't have broadband is cost,' explains Oliver Johnson, CEO of broadband consultancy Point Net. 'It's still expensive to buy all the kit you need, let alone the monthly subscription. Ironically, the cheapest rail fairs and the cheapest goods are online – meaning poorer people suffer twice over. One solution currently touted is mobile – as handsets are cheaper and you can pay as you go. But it's next to impossible to apply for Universal Credit on a mobile phone. The numbers are getting better but nowhere near as fast as people thought or hoped. What's left is a very long tail of digitally deprived people.'

The UK's Digital by Default programme – involving moving twenty-five government services, from voter registration to driving licence application, entirely online, effectively excludes these one in five digitally deprived households. Significantly, Universal Credit – which is gradually replacing Jobseeker's Allowance – is a digital-only service. It's rolling out around the country with a target that all new claimants will be on Universal Credit by September 2018. Existing claimants on other benefits will be transferred to Universal Credit between July 2019 and March 2022. Universal Credit will amount to £53 billion by 2020–1, with almost half of families with children entitled to it. Only the state pension will be bigger.

When Universal Credit was first mooted by Iain Duncan Smith's Centre for Social Justice in 2010, it was designed to replace six existing benefits, including Jobseeker's Allowance and Tax Credits, to simplify the benefits system, ease entry into work and improve earnings incentives by allowing families to keep more of each additional pound earned. Hence, it was welcomed by charities like Oxfam for its attempt to adapt the benefit system to the more chaotic employment market of the post-industrial world.

Beveridge's social insurance – or unemployment benefit – had been designed for the post-war world where people had long-term jobs punctuated by brief periods of unemployment. Today, especially in lower-paying roles, employment is sporadic and fitful, with regular periods on benefits in-between contracts. This causes problems: alongside unemployment benefit there's a whole package of different benefits such as housing benefit, child benefit and Jobseeker's Allowance, all of which come on and off stream at different rates as people jump between jobs or take part-time work, in some cases making getting a job entirely pointless.

Take Jack, a bricklayer I met in Bradford who's been looking for work for two years. Jack made a good living in London during the 1990s and early 2000s before heading to Germany on the offer of a lucrative contract in 2007. He was out there for a few years but came back as the recession bit. He's taken a fork-lift truck operator course and can get a week's work here and there – when he first got back he worked on a couple of house refurbishments but the brief contracts meant he had to sign off, then sign on again, relatively quickly. This played havoc with his housing benefit – he'd sometimes miss a couple of months' rent thanks to the inconsistency. In the end, short contracts meant he was more likely to lose his one-bedroom flat and end up at a hostel.

Universal Credit was designed to overcome this chop-and-change life and make it easier for people to manage short contracts or badly paid jobs and still go to work. The broad principle is that it guarantees you a basic income – which it pays monthly rather than weekly – and covers housing costs. For a single person under twenty-five, Universal Credit pays £251.77 a month, or £3,021.24 per year. Those over twenty-five get £317.82, or £3,813.84 per year. A couple over twenty-five get £498.98 per month, or £5,987.76 per year.

If Jack was on Universal Credit and found work, his claim stays open. If the work pays less than Universal Credit, it tops up. The original design of Universal Credit significantly improved the incentive to start work at a job with short hours. For instance, a home-owning single parent could work twenty-two hours per week before seeing their benefits reduced.

In the summer budget of 2015, however, Universal Credit was changed significantly. The maximum number of hours worked before benefits reduce dropped from twenty-two to ten, meaning work will pay on average £1,000 less. The rate at which benefits are reduced means families will lose 65p of each additional pound they earn. If their income rises to above the income tax threshold, this increases to 76p.

In February 2016, in the face of rising protests, the chancellor, George Osborne, scrapped planned cuts to Working Tax Credits – but retained cuts to Universal Credit. As a result, people on Universal Credit became worse off than those on traditional benefits. A low-earning single parent working sixteen hours a week at £9 an hour earns – with tax credits – £278 a week. Under Universal Credit they will be £29 a week worse off.

As Universal Credit is digital only, claimants are expected to make their applications and manage any subsequent changes online – all relevant contact between the DWP and the claimant will be done via the internet. Jobcentres do provide free Wi-Fi and more than 6,000 job-search terminals nationwide, according to the DWP, 'with staff providing additional support if needed so benefit claimants can look for and apply for jobs'.

With unemployment standing at 1.6 million at the end of 2016, however, it's clear that 6,000 terminals can't service all those who need to be online between ten and thirty-five hours each week. And in a remarkable piece of institutional doublethink, the government announced in January 2017 that it would close one in ten Jobcentres. Damian Hinds, the minister for employment, said the closures reflected today's welfare state as 'people increasingly claim benefits online'. Jobcentres may offer Wi-Fi and free job-search terminals to help people get online, but people are increasingly accessing welfare online so they're closing the Jobcentres.

Even if the Jobcentres weren't closing, it's not a simple business to access one of the terminals. 'You can't just walk in to the Jobcentre and use the computers, you have to make an appointment,' explains Andrew Young, research and campaigns officer at Newcastle Citizens Advice Bureau.

> It's frustrating to have to book that time – especially if you're going to be sanctioned for not searching. We had one client who was homeless and couldn't get an appointment to use the computer but the Jobcentre insisted he apply online. They told him to use the library – but you need an address to apply for a library card.

In other words, with the lowest-earning 20 per cent of the country having limited, restricted or no access to broadband,

Universal Credit is a benefit system available to only the richest 80 per cent of the country. It's an outright destruction of the principles behind helping those worse off get back on their feet. And there's a dark additional feature to Universal Credit introduced in the summer 2015 budget: the demands placed on jobseekers have been extended to the low paid, through an unprecedented 'in-work conditionality' rule.

People working fewer than thirty-five hours per week at the national living wage, including claimants who may never have been on the dole in their life but have had Working Tax Credits, child tax credits or help with housing costs, are forced to attend Jobcentre interviews on a weekly or fortnightly basis. They must also spend several hours a week applying for second jobs online, as a condition for receiving low-wage pay top-ups. If they break this commitment, they face sanctions.

So a toxic lack of access to basic communications means food and housing could be threatened for the digitally deprived. Rebecca is thirty-six and lives within sight of the boarded-up Ford factory gate in Speke, Liverpool. She was sanctioned because her laptop broke and she couldn't get access to another computer for one day. 'You can apply for a crisis loan after a week,' she explained, 'but that has to be over the phone, takes about two hours and it's not free from a mobile number. I've got no money, I've got to be on the phone two hours for the application and being sanctioned I can't always afford to top the mobile phones up. Most people on benefits don't actually have a landline.'

Figures on how many pay-as-you-go customers regularly run out of credit are vague. The UK has 36.1 million pre-pay users, according to Ofcom figures, although no company will release exact figures on how many have zero credit at any one time. A source at one mobile phone company suggested this runs at around 30 per cent, 'but it's hard to be sure exactly why they've got a zero balance', he explains. So there are some 10 million people who are unable to make calls or access their answerphone at any one time.

For Leona in Sheffield, running out of pre-pay meant she struggled to get much-needed medical help. 'I was sick with something I didn't understand and I didn't have the money to phone my GP to get an appointment,' she explains. 'The practice won't take walk-ins. I had to ask my neighbour to phone the doctor for me and make an appointment.'

And for those who can afford broadband, there's a final divide – broadband quality. In 2014, Ofcom surveyed broadband speeds in eleven UK cities and found wide variations in speed by region and district. For example, people in Cardiff and Inverness were twice as likely to be on a slower connection than those in London or Birmingham, and superfast broadband was less widely available in those parts of cities with lower incomes, with 57.8 per cent of homes and business in the poorest parts of Glasgow having access to superfast broadband compared to a national average of 90 per cent.

The differences between urban and rural speed – as measured in 2016 – were more significant still: average download speeds in rural areas were 13.7 Mbps, while those in urban areas were more than three times that, at 50.5 Mbps. There's a deep digital divide between the better off/better connected and the rest of the country.

For Nick, the strain of bouncing from home to library to Jobcentre to skills course is starting to show. He's always been friendly and sociable and he's feeling cheerful today, but he's started to feel miserable every time he climbs the library stairs or walks into the Jobcentre. 'You can see all these gloomy faces – no one wants to be there, I don't want to be there,' he says quietly. 'If I get sanctioned again it'll be for longer – how do they expect you to pay for stuff? It's like they're pushing you to go and commit crime.'

Nick East feels the unemployment system is a bewildering and mendacious bureaucracy that's actively trying to take money away from him rather than guiding him towards a sustainable job. He's probably right. In 2015, John Longden, a personal adviser at Salford Jobcentre Plus and Rochdale Jobcentre Plus between 2011 and 2013, gave evidence to Parliament regarding the pressures on staff to deliver a minimum number of sanctions per week. Longden was instructed to 'agitate' and 'inconvenience' customers and told, 'Let's set them up from day one.' Customers were sent to all job programmes regardless of their suitability. Decision Making and Appeals hit squads scrutinised job searches at an almost forensic level, looking to find a reason for suspension of benefit. Customers had to apply for a minimum of six jobs per week, regardless of their skills or experience. Customers were told to attend the Jobcentre daily – in the hope, according to Longden, that they would miss an appointment or be late, resulting in benefits being suspended or the claim being closed.

Langdon also discovered that his and other adviser appointments were being booked by the office manager without informing the customer, claiming the customer had been notified in person with a letter by hand, even though this could not have been the case.

The stupidity of sanctions around the country suggest Langdon may actually have worked at one of the kinder Jobcentres. In Brighton, a fifty-eight-year-old woman who had been unemployed for seven months was told that she had to travel miles to work in a Scope charity shop in Worthing or lose her benefits. She couldn't afford to get to Worthing, so she offered to work in the Scope shop in Brighton, but the Jobcentre wouldn't allow it. She was sanctioned.

And there is, astonishingly, no actual proof that sanctions work – at least not in the way they were intended. In November 2016, the National Audit Office (NAO) estimated that in 2015 the DWP spent £30–50 million a year applying sanctions, around £200 million monitoring the conditions it sets for claimants, and paid out £35 million in hardship payments. Over the year, the NAO said, the department withheld £132 million from claimants in sanctions. This meant the programme was in the red by some £150 million. If that net loss produced positive results getting Britons back to work, of course, that would have been worthwhile.

Research from the ESRC in May 2016 suggested that bene-fit sanctions – especially severe sanctions – did raise exits from benefits, and may have increased short-term job entry, although the longer-term outcomes for earnings, job quality and long-term employment were largely unfavourable.

Helping claimants into secure employment isn't working, researchers found, but they noticed heightened vigilance from jobseekers and a greater attention to detail in meeting the demands of conditionality – they arrived for appoint-ments earlier and applied for jobs they did not have adequate qualifications for, to show they applied for the minimum number of jobs for that fortnight. Sanctions are essentially making people better at applying for benefits. The ESRC also identified a significant number of sanctioned claimants who were disconnecting from both welfare and work, turning to petty crime or black market cash jobs.

In Hartlepool I met Callum, a volunteer at a local youth centre. He's slim and pale and looks younger than his twenty-one years. He can pass for under sixteen on buses roughly half the time, he says with a shamefaced grin. Austerity has been tough on Hartlepool – the town's population of 92,000 had lost £28.9 million as a result of public spending cuts by the end of 2015 – a drop of 24.5 per cent since 2010 according to the Association of North East Councils. Dyke House estate – where Callum grew up and where two-bedroom terraced houses are on sale for £20,000 – is in the top 1 per cent of Britain's Index of Multiple Deprivation. With 197 crimes per 1,000 people, and 97 of those for antisocial behaviour, the area scores higher than the national average of 102 and 35 respectively – as well as the northeast average of 121 and 59.

Walking through the estate's low-rise old- and new-build houses, however, the streets don't feel unsafe. Callum showed me the gaps between buildings, empty sites left bare by a housing renewal programme that now host surly groups of teenagers as the evening comes. There were some signs of petty vandalism. Mostly, however, the streets were deserted. No children played, no neighbours chatted, no cars came through as we wandered around.

'In this area you don't get many people with jobs – in my family there's been a lot of unemployment,' Callum explained as we walked. 'I don't want to be like that, I want to work. I just think life's what you make of it. Like, you have to do the best you can, and if you can't do the best you can then just go along with it – because there's no point giving up. Then you'll just have a negative impact in life really won't you? But I always think positive about things. If something happens I'll just think about the positive stuff, not the negative – if I think about the negative then it will have an impact on me, and that's something I don't like.'

He lives with his dad and two brothers. His mum 'cares for me nanna because she's going to die. She lives down the side of the mosque – where it used to be a shop at the bottom of that street? That was me nanna's shop – me granddad passed away seven years ago and me nanna's not been the same since.' Callum's house isn't too far from his mum – and it's a big step up from his previous place – 'there's druggies that used to live next door, and when they were high they'd just come in . . . not fighting but starting arguments and stuff and I was sick of it.'

His dad and one brother are signing on – his other brother, however, has disconnected completely after being sanctioned. He no longer claims any benefits and survives on cash-in-hand sweeping-up jobs and lottery scratch card wins. At the time I met Callum he was getting by on a £40 win – 'If I said to him, "You're living in poverty," he'd just laugh at me.' Callum shrugged. 'He'd be like, "No, I'm all right." He won't see what he's doing until he's in his early fifties and he's one of the others that die in this area in their early fifties . . . and even then I don't think he would realise that it was linked at all to where he grew up.'

Other people on the estate have similarly disappeared from the Jobcentre, taking odd jobs for cash in places like Dalton Street – packed with car mechanics – or selling their possessions and, in some cases, stuff they've robbed on Facebook pages like 'A Quid for a Bid with Reserve, Hartlepool', where you can pick up prom dresses, Star Wars toys, broken Samsung Galaxy S6s and kids bikes for tiny sums.

There's also a flourishing black market health economy. Callum has known people trade antibiotics – having taken a few and felt better they then sell them on. One near neighbour sells on his prescription drugs for heartburn to any neighbour with indigestion. Sometimes Callum's dad takes a few – his stomach bothers him so much he can be doubled up with pain, unable to move. On a recent visit to the doctors – right across town – he was told it was something to do with the flu. 'I said to him, I said you need to see a different doctor – because you can tell it's not the flu,' Callum explains. 'He's in so much pain . . . But he just buys the pills.'

Despite this unpromising background, Callum volunteers at the youth club for eighteen hours a week – and has done since he was eighteen. He also attends college part-time, studying for a City and Guilds certificate in Children and Young People's Development, with the aim of working with young offenders. It's an area he has some personal experience of – there have been a couple of family members who served time. He is working through level two but will have to retake his GCSEs in maths and English to reach level three. 'I think maths is easy, I enjoy it, but I don't really enjoy English,' he shrugged, as we sat down in a room in the youth centre.

You'd be hard put to find anyone of any background more determined to change their position in life, turning up every day to volunteer despite his mates' incredulous mocking, and studying hard to improve his prospects. And yet, in May last year, Callum was sanctioned for nine months for missing an interview that his work coach had told him not to attend. 'She was like, "No, just leave it out and I'll sort it out," and then they sanctioned me . . . I said, I'd been told not to go there.' He shrugged again. 'It made no difference. They get a bonus if they sanction someone.'

He's been getting some hardship payments and his extended family have chipped in, while the youth centre gives him £20 per week towards his college fees, notepads and pens 'which I needed badly', he admitted. 'I know I need to do uni to work in juvenile and I'm hoping to. But they don't really like me being unavailable for work through college and volunteering, so maybe something has to give.'

Searching for work via the Universal Jobmatch has proved spectacularly fruitless. He's mandated to job search for a minimum seventeen hours a week, but has 'literally never had one interview from that site yet', he explained. 'The only interviews I've had – like some work as a community researcher – have been when I've applied for jobs through the youth centre. Hopefully if I keep at it something will come up and I'll get paid work . . . You have to try, right?'

8

Ignorance – Unreported

Ignorance is an evil weed which dictators may cultivate among their dupes but which no democracy can afford among its citizens.

Sir William Beveridge, *Full Employment in a Free Society*

'The British media needs to take responsibility for its behaviour over the past ten years,' Stephen Ellis, producer of the Shelter-backed documentary series *Slum Britain*, said at its London launch event in December 2016. 'It has systematically misreported, demonised, insulted and mocked those least able to speak for themselves.' Ellis, who had spent the previous couple of years covering the war in Syria, was shocked at the disparity between the media image of low-income families, temporary accommodation and homelessness and the reality he found when making the series. It was, he said, as if we'd been lied to.

When the images we have of each other are hugely distorted, it becomes easier to objectify and vilify others. When groups of people are missing from our national narrative, it's easier to ignore them. Gradually, as a nation, the UK is drifting apart – the centre focuses on its own self-image and those outside London feel ignored, overruled, undermined and detached. In the past, there was an umbilical link between the regions and the centre – local MPs went to Westminster to argue for their constituents and local newspapers covered local events, but also produced generation after generation of journalists who moved to the national media after cutting their teeth covering council estates, council meetings and local fetes.

But today MPs are parachuted in by the national party, and local papers are disappearing fast. December 2016 figures from the *Press Gazette* show some 198 local newspapers closed in the UK between 2005 and the end of 2016 (with forty-six of those closing in 2015–16) as the country's big four local media groups – Trinity Mirror, Newsquest, Local World and Johnston Press – cut costs in the face of declining advertising revenue.

When, in 2009, the Welsh steel town of Port Talbot lost its last local paper, the *Port Talbot Guardian*, Rachel Howells, a former journalist turned PhD researcher, decided to investigate the effects. Port Talbot's industrial history is one huge cycle of boom and bust. Built on steel (iron-making in this part of South Wales dates back to the thirteenth century), at its peak in the 1960s the Port Talbot works employed nearly 20,000 people and the town enjoyed virtually full employment. Wages were so high it was nicknamed Treasure Island and was the first place in Wales to have a casino. There was even an attempt to rob the bank in the 1960s because the payroll for the steel-workers was so large – a team of Cardiff-based criminals tried to dig under Station Road and into the vault at the Midland Bank.

During the good years, there were five newspapers with an office in town – the *Evening Post*, *Port Talbot Guardian*, *South Wales Echo*, *Western Mail* and *Courier*. As many as eleven journalists worked there, competing for scoops and covering courts, council meetings, public meetings, protests, conferences, accidents and everyday community life. 'I found they used to have beat reporters who would literally be out on the street, walking down roads and chatting to people about what was going on in the town,' Howells says when we meet in a café overlooking the derelict skeleton of an ancient warehouse. 'They'd be out finding stories from housewives or people in cafés. That's a proper ear to the community. But the sad fact is that the number of journalists working in Port Talbot has fallen more than 90 per cent in the last forty years.'

The town slowly declined as the steel industry shrank. The derelict Plaza Cinema is a grim patchwork of neglect and decay decorated with tatty murals of the town's most famous sons – Michael Sheen, Richard Burton and Sir Anthony Hopkins – which surround broken windows and soot-smudged walls. The local papers drifted away as the town got smaller and poorer, and when the *Guardian* closed the community lost a crucial source of information.

This has caused a number of problems. Take, for instance, the closure of Port Talbot's junction with the M4 – Junction 41. The M4 soars above Port Talbot on a huge concrete flyover and, with Port Talbot Parkway station, is the main way in and out of town. The Welsh Assembly began discussing the closure of the motorway slip road in the same year the

Guardian closed. There were concerns about congestion at peak time slowing journey time to West Wales – possibly coincidentally, the Welsh Assembly economy and transport minister at the time, Edwina Hart, commuted along the M4 between the Gower peninsula and the Cardiff-based Assembly.

Eventually, in March 2014, the Assembly decided on a trial closure during rush hour on August 4. The first time most locals realised they could no longer access the motorway during rush hour came when they found men in high-vis vests behind rows of traffic cones blocking their way. Chaos ensued. The local council told protestors that it had put up information posters, some in the Civic Offices and some in the Aberafan Shopping Centre, but Howells was researching local news in Port Talbot at the time, talking to focus groups and community groups, and no one had received any information. One man only realised something was amiss when an anonymous graffiti artist spray painted 'Save J41' on the motorway's concrete buttresses.

Talking to a group of young men, irate about the politicians' casual disregard for feelings in the town, Howells was alarmed. 'They were so angry that I was shaking when I left the room,' she said. 'When they first built the M4 through the centre of Port Talbot, it tore the town in two. They did that against local objections as well. Then they've cut off our access to it – which feels like the final insult. There was a palpable feeling that if they weren't listened to, they'd have to make themselves heard.'

Mike Hutin, who led the 'No to the Junction 41 Closure' campaign, remembers the value of the *Port Talbot Guardian*. Back in 2001, his son Andrew was killed in a blast furnace explosion at the town's steelworks – now owned by Tata Steel, but then owned by Corus. The local paper covered the tragedy in depth and helped keep pressure on Corus to make safety improvements. After the paper closed, he explained, he found it harder to get people along to monthly Junction 41 protest meetings and found it harder to pick up stories from other people affected by the junction's closure.

Elsewhere, Jeremy Bailey led one local residents' group protesting at the building of the world's largest biomass plant in the town. Port Talbot already has four power stations and one huge steel factory. Air pollution is a serious problem: westerly winds can raise pollution to nine on the governments ten-point air quality index, and black dust pollution from the steelworks led to an enforcement notice from Natural Resources Wales as recently as 2013. Biomass plants can cause significant emissions of nitrogen dioxide and particulates as well as toxic dioxins and furans.

'There's different levels to a campaign,' Bailey explains. 'First you've got leaflets – that gets you a meeting of concerned residents. But then, if you're going to take things on, you need the local media. One of the *Port Talbot Guardian*'s journalists lived round the corner from me – he took an interest in the campaign, took time to understand the issue and the paper covered us on the front page and opened up the letters page to debates on the plant.'

That thoughtful analysis also meant Friends of the Earth, who were broadly pro-biomass, took the Port Talbot protest more seriously. The regional paper, the *South Wales Evening Post*, based in Swansea, was not as thorough. 'They were only interested in covering marches or rallies – although they told us they didn't have the staff to cover marches on

Saturdays, so could we organise them mid-week?' he recalls. The protest group pushed for a judicial review – but the costs incurred were huge and Jeremy began a desperate round of fundraising. Halfway through, the *Port Talbot Guardian* closed and he noticed it instantly became harder to raise interest and cash. 'Local papers are part of the voice of the community,' Bailey argued. 'Closing them takes away our chance to be heard.'

'There's a real democratic value in having a local newspaper,' according to Dr Martin Moore, director of the Centre for the Study of Media, Communication and Power, and a senior research fellow in the Policy Institute at King's College London. 'It's not just that it allows the community to know what's going on. It's also that the presence of a journalist who turns up to council meetings makes local politicians more accountable and keeps tabs on their behaviour. As these papers close – or as they're hollowed out, closing local offices and running news-gathering from a hub in a city miles from people's lives – we're gradually creating a serious democratic deficit. There are now areas of the UK where there is virtually no professional news reporting at all.'

Port Talbot does get some coverage from the *South Wales Evening Post*, owned by Local World – although its circulation has declined in recent years from 36,623 in August 2012 to 22,572 in the first half of 2016, with just 3,000 copies sold in Port Talbot. The newsroom has also shrunk. 'In the last two years our newsroom has been reduced by about 15 per cent,' editor Jonathan Roberts told me, but insisted that 'papers or media groups are now able to create content in a different way'. Trinity Mirror, the owner of the *Western*

Mail, another regional paper which includes Port Talbot in its geographical reach, 'fundamentally disagreed' that there had been a decline in local news coverage. In a written statement after I approached them, Trinity Mirror said,

> We are comfortable that changes are not impacting the quality or depth of news coverage in local areas but rather they are adapting to shifts in society, and the changes in how, where and when people want to get local news. Failing to adapt by continuing to try to push a twentieth-century product to a twenty-first-century world would be significantly more damaging.

It's true there's a risk of falling into the golden age versus digital evangelist argument – which, Moore argues, is missing the point. 'It's not about the survival of print or the problems with digital – it's that it's proved very hard to sustain day-in day-out reporting if you have a volunteer team,' he argued. 'You need professional journalists holding people to account and it doesn't matter which medium they're doing that in. There used to be a career route for young reporters on local papers to move to nationals, bringing regional knowledge and a respect for their area. Now there are many national journalists who skip that stage altogether – which is one of the reasons the national media and to some extent Westminster itself can seem out of touch with the rest of the country.'

There's no official measure of the impact of local newspaper closures across the UK, but there is, as near as possible, some measurable proof from the USA regarding the damage to local democracy when a newspaper closes. On New Year's Eve 2007, the Ohio-based *Cincinnati Post* closed, leaving the

Cincinnati Enquirer as the city's sole daily newspaper. The *Post*'s final publication date had been fixed thirty years previously – the *Enquirer* had part-funded its rival since the 1970s under a local monopoly ruling – meaning Sam Schulhofer-Wohl, director of research at the Federal Reserve Bank of Minneapolis, could measure and rule out other possible influences on the subsequent changes in local politics.

'The year after the *Post* closed, voter turnout fell in the suburbs most reliant on the paper,' Schulhofer-Wohl explained over the phone. 'Fewer candidates ran for local office, incumbents became more likely to win re-election, and campaign spending fell – even though the *Enquirer* at least temporarily increased its coverage of the *Post*'s former patch.' Voter turnout remained depressed nearly three years after the *Post* closed, Schulhofer-Wohl reports. The project ended in 2011.

Howells tried to replicate a version of that study in Port Talbot but there weren't enough historic data – unlike in the USA, sample sizes for the area were small and she arrived as the *Port Talbot Guardian* closed. But she did find some evidence that backed the US studies. In 2000, all of the five newspapers but the *Port Talbot Guardian* closed their offices – and voter turnout started to fall. From 1970 to 1999, the local Aberavon constituency had a voter turnout on average 2.5 per cent higher than the UK average. The 2004 local elections were the first to show the drop – turnout was 0.7 per cent below the UK average, and fell to 4 per cent below in 2010.

'One of the journalists I spoke to told me that people would come in off the street and say, "I've got a story for you," and if she said she was too busy, they said they were going down the road to get that newspaper to cover it,' Howells explains. 'That gave local people huge power and much more leverage to get their voices heard and represented, to get their issues out. Local people come to me now asking how to write a press release because the newspaper will only put our local rugby club in the paper if we send them photos and a match report. The journalists just have to sit in the office and write – the *Evening Post* has a journalist covering Port Talbot but he needs special dispensation to leave the office. That's really sad isn't it? Local rugby teams can't even put out the first fifteen these days – they don't get the numbers on the side-lines, and the lack of coverage must be a part of that. Those places that used to be vibrant hubs of the community are dying a death. Of course the lack of coverage is not the only reason, but it doesn't help.'

It's impossible to know how corrupt all the unreported councils are in the UK. Across the country, however, wherever hyper-local news operations – run by entrepreneurs, volunteers and academics and sometimes funded by charities in a bid to provide coverage in the absence of local media – are springing to life there are clear examples of corruption scandals broken by, and community campaigns lead by, these fledgling media outfits.

In Milford Haven, for instance, the *Pembrokeshire Herald* was launched by former lawyer Tom Sinclair in 2013, 'because for the previous thirteen years there was no real news coverage of the important issues in our county', he explained when we met in a quiet café. 'Pembrokeshire is covered by the *Western Telegraph* and the former publisher of the *Telegraph*, Len Mullins, is now the council's press officer. When a press release comes from the council, the

Telegraph prints a copy-and-paste version. There you go . . . that is the news. There is no scrutiny.'

Within months of its launch, the *Herald* claimed the scalp of Pembrokeshire county council Chief Executive Bryn Parry-Jones, the highest-paid council chief executive in Wales, with a salary of almost £195,000 plus benefits – including a Porsche leased as his work vehicle. In September 2013, the *Herald* revealed details of cash payments Parry-Jones was taking in lieu of pension contributions as part of a tax avoidance deal agreed at a private session of the council's senior staff committee. Parry-Jones resigned in October 2014 after the Wales Audit Office found the payments unlawful.

In Caerphilly, former *Brighton Argus* journalist Richard Gurner started the *Caerphilly Observer* in 2009 – initially online only, with a fortnightly print version launched in 2013 – after Newsquest, the group that owned the *Caerphilly Campaign*, closed its local office and ran the paper from Newport. 'They'd print a handful of Caerphilly stories at best and the rest came from Newsquest's other papers,' Gurner explained over the phone. 'There were no beat reporters in the town at all.' The *Observer* led a campaign against Caerphilly Chief Executive Anthony O'Sullivan and his deputy Nigel Barnett after they secured themselves pay rises worth tens of thousands of pounds. Following an investigation, the Welsh Audit Office ruled the pay rises unlawful, police arrested the men and they were suspended by the council. 'It's a local reporter who knows their own patch that drives stories like that,' according to Gurner.

Rachel Howells' solution to Port Talbot's democratic deficit was the *Port Talbot Magnet* – launched online in 2010 and rolling out to a quarterly print edition in September 2013 thanks to £10,000 from the Carnegie UK Trust. The paper rapidly became profitable, campaigning around the Afan Lido, a local leisure centre that burned down. The council was offering a substandard replacement until the *Magnet* and resident groups protested. The paper covered the J41 protests, and scrutinised Tata Steel — the town's main employer.

As you arrive in Port Talbot, Tata's steelworks dominate your view. It's spectacular at night; like the opening scene in *Blade Runner*, all winking lights, flares and alien structures. Coming in from the M4, it takes a good ten minutes to drive the full length of the works. Although it's a long way from the glory of its 1960s peak, until the start of 2016 Tata still employed 4,000 people, paying more than twice the minimum wage, and gave work to a further 10,000 through its supply chain. As a result Tata wields enormous local power and its actions often go uncontested.

The *Magnet* first took on Tata in 2011 when it highlighted collusion between Tata Steel and the local council to close off access to Morfa Beach — a wide, sandy beach popular with windsurfers and hikers. Tata's plans to close the footpath and part of the beach to the public had almost passed without notice until the *Magnet* picked up the story. Local protests led to a public inquiry, and in 2013 the footpath was saved. Other campaigns — around a dangerous abandoned quarry and the council withdrawing funding for Christmas lights — had similar results, and in May 2015, after months of pressure, the Welsh Assembly agreed to reopen Junction 41. 'It took us a really long time to gain people's awareness and then trust,' Howells explains. 'It took me five years to get on the local police mailing list. We never had a penny from the local council or Tata Steel. Eventually I was accepted into the hugely strong local community just by being around, but it took a really long time because Port Talbot has seen it all. They have seen people come in and have these wonderful ideas about projects and then they fall over and they go away. Nothing ever lasts and so I think they were a bit cynical.'

But just as the *Magnet* was gaining that trust, in January 2016 Tata Steel announced 750 job losses at the works. The icy economic winds this released hit the *Magnet* hard. Local business – cafés, shops, restaurants – all pulled their advertising. 'You can't blame them,' Howells says with a shrug. 'If you run a café and your husband is made redundant you want to save every penny you can.' January's edition was delayed but the paper carried on, publishing solid community stories such as how calls to the Samaritans had risen 30 per cent since the job cuts were announced. In March 2016 the team uncovered a 2014 application by Tata to recategorise the land the steelworks rest on as fit for residential development. The global forces Tata claimed were threatening the works – including the dumping of cheap Chinese steel on the international market – were not in evidence when the application was made.

That March, Tata announced it might close the works altogether. The national media descended on the bemused town for a frantic few days then vanished again. Shortly afterwards, an electrical fault at the plant lead to a controlled burning off of the gas used to heat the furnaces. National newspapers carried front page reports of a huge explosion rocking the steelworks. The *Magnet*, with its local connections, ran the correct story. 'You could have looked at Twitter and seen loads of exciting videos of all these flames, you could have read the *Daily Mail*, you could have read the *Express*, you could have read the BBC and read a dramatic version of events,' Howells grins. 'But if you're writing for an audience of steelworkers, you've got to know about steel, for God's sake. We need skilled individuals who can deal with information responsibly and accountably in a trustworthy position.'

In June 2016, a group of steelworkers approached her, worried about shortcuts to health and safety at the plant now that staff numbers had been reduced. They told her that manpower on some shifts was down by a third but that the same output was expected, that rest breaks had been cut so workers were now spending an hour in the full heat of the furnace with half an hour to cool off, meaning exhaustion and dehydration were increasingly common.

'It's a dangerous place,' the *Magnet* quoted one steelworker:

> If you don't treat it with respect every second of the day something will jump up and bite you. Now we're expected to do the job of a third more men than before – it's more draining, more tiring and we are less hydrated. That's when you get attention drift. But if something goes bang in there, you have to be on your toes and ready to evacuate. You can't take chances with hot strip metal shooting past you at 60 mph.

With the threat of closure, however, the *Magnet*'s advertising all but dried up completely. Eventually, in October, Howells had to call a halt. The final edition carried a front page story attacking government plans to reduce Welsh MP numbers and cut Port Talbot into two with boundary changes. Howells' farewell letter also carried a call to arms:

Port Talbot needs and deserves good quality news, but it must now come from you. Given time and dedication, a local news service can work. A host of small publishers are succeeding in print because they offer a truly local service, and have a willing audience who love what they do – and advertisers have followed. Unfortunately the Tata effect has stopped that from happening in Port Talbot for now. The *Magnet* is willing to hand over the website, the Facebook account and the Twitter account to local people, if someone will step up to take over. We can organise training and support through our contacts at Cardiff University's Centre for Community Journalism.

When we met in February 2017 there had been some tentative conversations with interested locals but nothing concrete. Howells sipped coffee and fretted over stories that kept coming in but that no one could cover any more; from a local charity closure to plans to redevelop a beach into retirement homes. 'Port Talbot is a small place with a small, precarious economy that struggled when Tata basically played the government because they didn't want to keep funding their pension plan.' She leans forward, urgently. 'It's the kind of place that needs local journalists. We've got to think about how we are going to pay for it, because the current model is broken but people can't participate in communities and in democracy effectively without some kind of general level of awareness.'

She quotes the two-step flow theory in communications, introduced by sociologist Paul Lazarsfeld in 1944 and incorporated into the bestselling book *The Tipping Point* by Malcolm Gladwell. It divides people into opinion leaders and opinion followers. A community thrives when there's a core group of people who know what's going on and then tell other people. If enough people finally know about an issue, everybody can have a decent conversation and make an informed decision. Remove the opinion leaders, reduce their numbers or withhold the facts from them and the general spread of knowledge stutters and dies.

In 2016, the Press Association reported that 57 per cent of voters in Neath Port Talbot had backed leaving the EU — when most predictions confidently assumed a narrow remain vote of 51 per cent. No one expected Port Talbot to vote leave because nobody had paid attention to the town for years. The UK is fragmenting into enclaves, divided by income and attitude, and we are no longer listening to each other. The consequences can be devastating for all of us.

9

Divided Kingdom

Freedom from want cannot be forced on a democracy or given to a democracy. It must be won by them. Winning it needs courage and faith and a sense of national unity: courage to face facts and difficulties and overcome them; faith in our future and in the ideals of fair play and freedom for which century after century our forefathers were prepared to die; a sense of national unity overriding the interests of any class or section.

Sir William Beveridge, *Social Insurance and Allied Services Report*

I arrived in Stoke on the day that local MP Tristram Hunt resigned. It was an event that excited less comment in the city itself than in the national media. The story was buried on page seven of Stoke's daily paper, the *Sentinel* – giving it lower billing than the opening of a CBeebies-themed attraction at nearby Alton Towers. The people who were discussing Hunt's departure assumed the United Kingdom Independence Party (UKIP) would dominate the by-election – either coming a very close second or winning the seat outright.

Labour has held the seat since it was created in 1950, but its majority dropped from nearly 20,000 a decade ago to just 5,000 in 2015, with UKIP coming second. This was a massive improvement for UKIP on results in 2010 when it trailed a poor fourth behind the three main parties and the British National Party. However, in February 2017 UKIP's leader, Paul Nuttall, ran a ham-fisted campaign and lost all advantage that might have been coming his way. Nevertheless, it was apathy that won the day in Stoke, with a turnout of just 36.69 per cent.

The gradual downwards slide of voter turnout in the city – 53.2 per cent in 2010, 49.9 per cent in 2015 – was briefly arrested by the EU referendum, where 70 per cent voted leave on a turnout of 65.7 per cent. This vote persuaded UKIP and most of the national papers to believe the 'Brexit capital of Britain' would bring Nuttall into Parliament. While he failed, he still managed to secure a 2.14 per cent swing from Labour to UKIP, cutting Labour's majority to 2,620.

Few experts can really say what went wrong, or right, in 2016's EU referendum. There has been a post-referendum scramble to understand why poorer, northern cities voted to leave the EU – it is vaguely understood in Westminster as a protest over immigration, but clearly this is not the whole reason. During the by-election campaign I spoke to a number of people in Stoke and it was clear that the EU vote – and more than a few potential UKIP votes – were directed as much, if not more, at Westminster as it was Brussels. 'There is a huge disconnect; the politicians haven't got any idea of what it is like outside London,' according to Alice James, who worked as a cleaner in one of the last potteries left in town. 'You can see that when they were so surprised at the referendum. None of them, especially the Labour Party, showed any understanding of white working-class people who had been hung out to dry, didn't have a lot of hope, had been excluded and shafted by power for years and years and years.'

Stoke itself is almost an accidental city. It is a collection of large towns running north to south along the A50 – Tunstall, Burslem, Hanley, Stoke-on-Trent, Fenton and Longton – all brought together in a grudging coalition in 1910. As a result, there's no city centre – each town has its own high street and own strong identity. Successive attempts to designate informally either Hanley or Stoke as the centre have been ferociously resisted, although the council, the bus station and the train station are all grouped around Stoke itself and Hanley boasts the largest shopping centre. To the west there's the slightly more upmarket Newcastle-under-Lyme. Along the eastern rim of the city, there's a collection of large council estates, roughly corresponding to the major pits, steelworks or potteries of the city's industrial peak.

There had been coal mines in the area as far back as the thirteenth century, and a huge pottery industry picked up in the seventeenth century – Royal Doulton, Spode, Wedgewood and Minton all started here. The first steelworks was built in the early 1800s. The coal heated the steel mill furnaces. The steel mills produced coke. Coke created the gas that fired the kilns. The industries were linked together in a complex ecosystem running down the Etruria Valley. When the steel mills started closing in 1972 – undercut by fuel subsidies for the German and French steel industries – the whole system slowly fell apart.

Today Stoke-on-Trent is the thirteenth most deprived city in England, with 34 per cent of working-age people living in households with incomes on or below the poverty line. More than 60,000 people live on less than £16,000 a year, the minimum amount needed to access basic goods and services. Around 15,000 households don't have an internet connection of any kind, 30,300 people have no qualifications at all, and nearly 30,000 people claim some form of out-of-work benefit. In 2014 residents of Hollings Street and Brocksford Street in Fenton told a police meeting that children had been rummaging through bins searching for and eating any food that had been thrown away.

A casual drive around Stoke can be bleak. One of the six towns – Burslem – has the highest retail vacancy rate in the country at 33.3 per cent, or one shop in three closed, against a UK average of 12.3 per cent. Along a side road opposite the Wedgewood Institute – an ornate gothic Victorian art college built in the 1860s and dedicated to Josiah Wedgewood – every shop window is covered by wooden boards. There's a derelict theatre and a closed down working men's club, and the street is practically deserted; just three people out on a Friday afternoon. Pictures from the 1970s and 1980s show a thriving town centre, pavements busy with shoppers and a range of stores from fashion boutiques to butchers shops open and trading. When the nearby potteries and factories closed, Burslem's daytime economy died.

'I think that's why Stoke voted to leave,' says Daniel Flynn of the local YMCA. 'The Remain people offered no hope for anybody – they just said "stay the same". If you're living in a shit council estate or somewhere the shops have all shut, why the hell would you want to stay the same? And when the middle classes kind of pooh-pooh you as ignorant, stupid people, sending us consultants to tell us we're bad parents or consultants to knock our houses down or consultants to tell us what an exciting regeneration project it is to build a park . . . it's no wonder half the country got more than a little pissed off.'

The United Kingdom has never been more divided. The Scottish independence referendum and the vote to leave the EU revealed the yawning gulf between Westminster and the rest of the country. In August 2016, the Joseph Rowntree Foundation analysed data from the British Election Study and found the poorest households, with incomes of less than £20,000 per year, were much more likely to support leaving the EU than the wealthiest households – as were the unemployed, people in low-skilled and manual occupations, people who feel that their financial situation has worsened and those with no qualifications. Those people who were the most likely to support Brexit were from areas that reported feeling 'left behind' – excluded and marginalised. 'Even if people possess educational qualifications and skills, if they are stuck in left-behind areas that are experiencing decline then they are less likely to be presented with local opportunities to use these skills and get ahead in life,' the Joseph Rowntree Foundation report's authors Matthew Goodwin and Oliver Heath argued. 'Such an environment can fuel feelings of exclusion or marginalisation.'

Across the big blue-collar leave-voting areas, this sense of isolation and resentment has been building for decades. Large council estates that once supported the Labour Party and believed in the democratic process are angry and disengaged. The old structures that reported local moods to central policymakers – including the local media – are falling away. Westminster misread the mood ahead of the Scottish referendum and, after polls suggested Yes would win, sent panicking cross-party delegations to promise the Scots everything if they'd stay. They thought remain was a shoo-in. The lines of communication are broken.

One ex-miner from the Dearne Valley in South Yorkshire explained how tiny acts of disrespect casually trampled over the community's wishes again and again and again. The Dearne Valley was once a rich coal seam and is dotted with villages usually built around the mouth of a pit. Since the mines have closed, it's now one of the most deprived parts of the UK – although residents could console themselves with bucolic views. Until the new-build houses for wealthy commuters blocked residents in. Until their own homes were bulldozed. Then the roads were built over football pitches in the name of redevelopment, and long-term unemployment was relieved briefly by short-term schemes underpinned by the perception in politics and the media that the residents' situation is ultimately their fault.

'There's a sense that the white working class is not being listened to that groups like the EDL [English Defence League] and UKIP tap into,' he explained. 'Politicians don't seem sure how to deal with it – cut down immigration is the only answer. But that's not the core reason. That's not really why people are angry. People want to be respected. They don't like being ignored. Over the last thirty years it's been lots of little things – this sense, with nothing to contradict you, that nobody cares what you say.'

In December 2016 I met Father Graeme Buttery, the vicar at St Oswald's Church, Hartlepool – a hearty man with a booming voice – in a community centre on the Dyke House Estate in Hartlepool. The town voted 70 per cent leave, and is the tenth most deprived local authority in the country, according to 2015's Index of Multiple Deprivation. Neighbouring Middlesbrough is the most deprived local authority in the UK. 'In the forty years since we've been members of the European Union, Hartlepool has seen the coal mines close, seen the steelworks rust, the fishing fleets sink, seen the chemical works explode and then they tried to tell us it would be a lot worse if we left,' Father Buttery explained. 'My parishioners – who are good folk – were angry about all sorts of things, but the vote wasn't some incoherent rage. It was a shout . . . please listen to us.'

Around the table with Father Buttery sat Malcolm Walker, a genial former steelworker who now works as a community organiser in Hartlepool, Alan Clark, who ran the town's biggest community-cum-leisure centre, and Peter Gowland, a local councillor. Walker had predicted his town's vote. 'We've got nothing,' he explains. 'If you've got nothing, you can't be scared by politicians telling you what you've got to lose. We've been in recession for the last thirty years. We know what it's like if we stayed – it's terrible.'

For Walker, the collapse of the pound is potentially a good thing for a town where, in September 2015, Thai-owned SSI closed the ninety-eight-year-old Redcar Steelworks, with the loss of 1,700 jobs, and July 2016 saw Tata Steel announce it would close or sell its remaining pipe mills. The weaker the pound gets, the more likely it is that British steel can compete with China on price and the plant might reopen,

Walker argues. If Scotland leaves the UK, he suggests, England will need somewhere to put the four Vanguard-class submarines that carry sixteen Trident missiles each, and Hartlepool has the deepest deep-water port on the North Sea. They're remote possibilities but at least they offer a possibility of hope. 'No one has offered us hope for a long time,' he explains.

Perhaps if it was only the industrial decline, Hartlepool wouldn't have rebelled so emphatically. Built on steel and shipbuilding, there were forty-three ship-owning companies in the town in 1913, with responsibility for 236 ships. So significant was the shipping industry that the first large German attack on the UK was directed against Hartlepool in December 1914, with three battle cruisers raining down 1,150 shells and killing 117 people. The last ship built in the town, the *Blanchard*, was launched in 1961. Through the late 1970s and into the 1980s, factories, steelworks and bottling plants were closed and pulled down. Back in the 1960s, the town's steel industry had employed 5,000 people. By the 1990s there were fewer than 1,200.

Unemployment and poverty have been high in Hartlepool ever since. The child poverty rate has been stuck at 30 per cent for years, unemployment stands at 10 per cent and in 2015 just over 27 per cent of homes – around 9,000 house-holds – had nobody over the age of sixteen working. Cuts to welfare have been brutal. Figures from the Association of North East Councils show that between 2010 and 2016 austerity cost the town £28.9 million. This is a 24.5 per cent drop worth £680 per household.

It's a town with a lot of fight. It has the largest number of start-ups in the region and youth unemployment is falling.

But the community keeps having parts of their identity chipped away. In 2016, Hartlepool lost control of its own police force as it merged with the Cleveland Police after the police commissioner removed the post of superintendent in Hartlepool. The local hospital has had services extracted over the past eight years until it's become a shell: just office space, one or two outpatient departments and the odd operation. The maternity unit was moved to Stockton in 2008; A&E services were transferred in 2011 followed by critical care; acute medicine and high-risk surgery moved in October 2013. 'If you're lucky they'll get you to Stockton, if you're unlucky – like one of my parishioners on Thursday – it's James Cook hospital in Middlesbrough, which is twelve miles away and difficult by public transport,' Father Buttery explains. 'It's really hit people that births now take place in Stockton – very few births are registered in Hartlepool, so most recent birth certificates say people are from Stockton. People aren't being born in Hartlepool anymore. I know some old people who've said, "If I have another stroke please just let me die at home." It's almost irrational but it's a feeling that the town's identity is being wiped out.'

It was the hospital that finally tipped the town into its current mood of wary rebellion. It came just after protestors from outside Hartlepool stopped a local firm decommissioning US navy ships for fear of contamination. 'There was a groundswell – not all of it necessarily justified – that we weren't being listened to and the town is powerless,' Alan Clark explains. 'The turnout for the referendum was higher than a general election. There were people going into polling booths with pens because they believed that people were going to rub their X out if they wrote it in pencil – people who'd never voted in their lives. The media like to whip up immigration as being the big problem – but if you look at Hartlepool it's 97 per cent white British. Immigration is not so much of a problem here. What there is – is frustration. Frustration because people can't get jobs, because the government will bail out the banks but they refused to save the steelworks, and there's this slow removal of chance and choice from a generation.'

This sense of social mobility slipping away creates fear more than anger. 'My father was a boilerman in a steelworks – his job was shovelling coal in a furnace,' Gowland explains. 'He had four sons – my eldest brother became a university lecturer, my second brother is a consultant engineer in the steel industry who travels the world building steelworks, the third one is a grammar school teacher and then there's me, the black sheep. They're full professionals, you know. I've been to visit a school this morning where 49 per cent of the children receive free school meals – and the teachers are having to feed the children when they go to school in the morning because they're not getting fed at home. How will those kids have those opportunities?'

The next day I met Ian Cawley, a big, bluff, genial man who runs the Heart Community Centre on the sprawling Owton Manor Estate. The centre sits at the end of a small parade of shops, next to a café and store called Jack's Essentials, which buys much of its inventory from the Facebook group 'A Quid for a Bid with Reserve, Hartlepool' mentioned earlier. Jack's Essentials promises 'no bike more than £30'. Lots of parents come in and put £10 down – some of them never return to pay the final £20 and pick the bike up.

Ian was the youngest of six and grew up in the late 1970s,

during Hartlepool's boom time, when the yards were open at Laing's, building huge oil rigs for the North Sea. His dad was a rigger and a union rep. The workforce was well organised and there were strikes – usually when they'd have the most effect. In 1977, there was a huge rig underway and the job wasn't getting done on time. The company said to Ian's dad, 'For every day ahead of deadline you get this rig out, we'll give everyone a £100 bonus.'

'My Dad said everybody was getting off their death bed just to get in there,' Ian recalls, laughing. 'I think he got just short of a £3,000 bonus – when you could buy a house round here for a couple of thousand pounds. We got a big family caravan with it. Then they had a party – it was legendary . . . they got the rig out and it was one of the first and the fastest ever. People just stood in the streets to watch it get towed out. There were wagons with crate-loads of whisky – they were hauling the drunks to safety.'

By the time Ian left school in 1986 the boom was over. There were no jobs. He did two years' labouring in an engineering workshop, was made redundant and went to sign on for the first time. It was raining, and he was half an hour early so he went into the army careers office next door. 'They said, "Which part of the army do you want to join?" I said, "Is there parts? What does that even mean?" "Well," they said, "for the paras you have to do twice as many pull ups." I went for less pull ups and ended up in the King's Division, the Green Howards.'

He did six tours in Northern Ireland – three in Londonderry, two in Armagh and one in Belfast. He was in the Falklands, Kenya, Cyprus, Germany, Chile, the Cayman Islands, Panama and Miami and then he left, aged twenty-three, to work on building sites, mainly doing concrete mixing. He worked for the engineering firm Amec in Hartlepool – 'doing mechanical fittings, pipefitter's mate and stuff like that' – then worked as a community warden, 'which was like policing on the cheap. Blunkett's Bobbies we were called and that was alright.' He ended up as a truancy officer on the Owton Manor Estate. The first house he went into with the social worker, the kids only had 7 per cent attendance. 'The social worker said, "This is one of the bad ones,"' he recalls. 'I said I'd already seen bad houses – I used to knock doors down in Londonderry and Belfast and we'd see things. She said, "No, this is one of the worst houses you'll see" . . . and she wasn't wrong.'

The house stank: 'You could see there was piss and shite and it was just . . . the stench and the stink and the state of the two people who were bringing these kids up. Bright as a button, these kids were. You think – how can this be allowed?' And he decided to set up the Heart Community Centre shortly after because he could see the estate was in danger of falling apart.

With the effect of benefit sanctions, people were turning to scams and petty crime. The more legitimate schemes were things like drop shipping – where people buy lists of suppliers online and take on small shipping consignments for them, making a few pounds profit on the delivery. There's a black market in everything from stolen cheese to cannabis. There are, he explains, hundreds of cannabis-growing houses in Hartlepool. 'They're generating twenty to thirty thousand pounds every three months and that's supporting the families,' he shrugs. 'Most of them grow and sell bulk. It's becoming an entire economy, things like that, because what else is there? No one bats an eyelid – they've cut that many police officers, none of them come through an estate like this.'

Those that aren't operating in the grey economy are struggling. The woman he was speaking to as I walked in has no bed at home – she sleeps on the floor. She fled an abusive relationship, eventually got an unfurnished flat and she's been buying odd bits and pieces of furniture when she can. Just before I arrived, she was telling him – full of excitement – about a friend of hers taking her out to eat the night before. They went to Kentucky Fried Chicken: 'Can you imagine it?' she said, as if it was the grandest adventure in the world. 'Me? In KFC? I felt about six feet tall.' But she's the first to volunteer if he's looking for help and she never complains about her life.

The Heart has a small computer room for the people on Universal Credit and Ian offers advice to people having trouble filling in forms. 'The people who are really uneducated, can't fill their forms out, can't do what's asked of them, can't get online to do the computers – they're pretty hard on them, the Jobcentre,' he explains. 'They're the first to be sanctioned. Lots of people round here don't eat at certain times, or certain parts of the week. They always say they're not hungry.'

With the local hospital cutting back, he set up something called the Big League, encouraging groups of neighbours to form a team that all go in and get weighed individually. Each week, anyone losing weight, anyone putting on events around health and community, anyone getting involved scores points for the team. At the end of the 'season' there was £1,000 worth of clothes vouchers for the winning team.

He's also set up a Time Exchange in which sixty-two volunteers help local charities, doing odd jobs, shopping for the elderly, going round to hold a ninety-three-year-old lady's hand, light-bulb changing, a little bit of painting: 'We're calling it self-interest volunteering,' he explains. 'If you volunteer for us for an hour we pay you 10 Poolie pounds, which you can spend at the centre on a professional CV, a suit for an interview, car hire if you need to get to a job interview, even CSCS [Construction Skills Certification Scheme] cards to get work on the building sites.'

The aim of the Beveridge Report was to stop the kind of desperate need that Cawley's centre still encounters on a daily basis. He believed the nation could and would pull together to make the country a much better place for everyone to live. Instead, thanks to the determined restructuring of the economy, we're divided along so many more lines than Beveridge could have imagined – race, class, gender, money, poverty, geography, attitude and even mobility.

The ending of social mobility is perhaps the greatest sign of the report's failure. When Beveridge talked about mobility, he meant the chance to improve your lot through education and better jobs. Today, as the industrial towns died, mobility means moving away.

Some have moved and others have stayed. There's a saying that it takes a whole village to bring up a child; in the case of Hartlepool, the town seems like a gentle but weary parent, doing its best to keep its children warm. In places like Hartlepool, the jobs used to be hard and dangerous. People worked for their families and they developed the camaraderie that warriors share when they stand together in peril. They have a shared history – a sense of place and belonging – which you can't buy, and when it's taken away you can't replace. This is the place where they were born. If you make it all but impossible for their children to be born in Hartlepool, you're taking away their identity – the one thing they had that can't be bought or sold. It's no wonder they're angry.

'There's a feeling that everything is failing – even the church is failing what the Bishop would call "estates people",' says Father Buttery. 'We're retreating from the estates for all sorts of reasons – demographics, decline in numbers, and the huge difficulty of getting clergy to come north. My folk, my congregation, know that. So what's left is community. No political party, no government, no bishops, no lords care about this town. So fair enough, it's the community alone. We'll show you what we can do.'

10

More than Half the Sky

The census includes married women who do not work for money outside their homes among unoccupied persons. The unemployment insurance scheme recognises such women as adult dependants on their husbands, in respect of whom the benefit of the husband is increased if he is unemployed. The health insurance scheme does not recognise such women at all, except at the moment of maternity. None of these attitudes is defensible.

Sir William Beveridge, *Social Insurance and Allied Services Report*

The first time Imani used a food bank came about when her son's school liaison officer came to investigate his absence over the past few days. Imani had served in the Royal Navy, become pregnant soon after leaving and had settled in London with a small relocation budget. She got a job cleaning at a large London university – working for a contracted-out cleaning company, and taking home minimum wage. Towards the end of 2016 the cleaning company changed its shifts and with the other cleaners, Imani was told she would need to work from 7.00 am till 9.00 am, go home, then come back in for 4.00 pm till 7.00 pm, a cut in hours, a resulting cut in salary and a doubling of her travel costs.

In the last few weeks of the Christmas term she found herself running out of food. She couldn't afford a packed lunch for her son and she couldn't afford to pay for school dinners. So she phoned him in sick and asked a neighbour to help her look after him while she worked. When the school liaison officer eventually referred her to the food bank, she confesses quietly, 'I felt so ashamed . . . it's like, I couldn't even feed my boy. I felt like a terrible parent.'

There are around 2 million single parents – making up 25 per cent of families with children, a figure that's stayed constant for a decade. Nine out of ten single parents are women – with less than 2 per cent of those being teenagers; 66.5 per cent of single parents are in work, but single-parent families are nearly twice as likely to be in poverty as those in two-parent families. In November 2016, research from the single-parent charity Gingerbread showed single parents of a young child made up more than half of households affected by the autumn benefit cap, which meant that affected families faced an average shortfall of £60 a week in rent. One single mother from Swansea phoned the charity's helpline in tears after receiving a letter from the DWP saying her benefits would be cut by £50 a week, while a divorced mother of three from Oxfordshire lost £126 a week.

In any study of low incomes in the UK, it's clear that women have been far harder hit by austerity and changes to social care. Analysis by the Women's Budget Group shows tax and benefit changes since 2010 will have hit women's incomes twice as hard as men by 2020. House of Commons figures show that, by 2020, 81 per cent of the £82 billion in cuts announced since 2010 will disproportionately affect women, meaning women will be £1,003 a year worse off by 2020 on average; for men, this figure is £555. Less-affluent women will be the worst affected: those with below-average incomes will find themselves £1,678 worse off. And black minority ethnic women are the hardest hit of all. Over 40 per cent of Bangladeshi and Pakistani children are growing up in poverty, compared with 31 per cent of Chinese, 22 per cent of Black Caribbean and 15 per cent of white children, according to Joseph Rowntree Foundation figures.

One in four women are in low-paid and insecure work, often receiving about 18 per cent less per hour than men in equivalent jobs. This gap widens consistently for twelve years after a first child is born, by which point women typically receive 33 per cent less per hour than men. Women are far more likely to be self-employed and work part-time: two-thirds of people who work for themselves on a part-time basis are women. This lowers pay further, as the gender pay gap for the self-employed is around 41 per cent. The average net income of female pensioners per week is approximately 85 per cent of their male counterparts, and over two-thirds of pensioners living in poverty are women.

The severe cuts that austerity has inflicted on council budgets – local authorities in England lost 27 per cent of their real-terms spending power between 2010–11 and 2015–16 – have not been evenly distributed. In England, the most deprived authorities saw cuts of more than £220 per head compared with under £40 per head for the least deprived, according to analysis by the Joseph Rowntree Foundation. This has produced a lurching inequality in social care spending – spending has risen by £28 per head, or 8 per cent, in the least deprived areas, but it has fallen in the most deprived areas by £65 per head, or 14 per cent. Council funding will be further reduced by 6.7 per cent between 2016 and 2020, with the bulk of the cuts frontloaded in the first two years. Councils have sought to ring-fence advice, social work and housing services – meaning services women rely on have suffered.

Across the country, services for children and young people have been reduced, including after-school activities, holiday clubs, play centres and youth clubs, while 17 per cent of women's refuges closed due to funding cuts between 2010 and 2016, despite two women being killed every week by domestic violence.

Many of the refuges that remain open have been forced to reduce capacity. A Women's Aid survey found that 6,337 of the 20,000-plus women looking for help at a refuge were turned away in 2016. And this is increasing. In 2016, 48 per cent of domestic violence services in England were running without any funding. In Sunderland, Cumbria and Devon there are no refuges left.

Funding cuts for social care have also hit sexual health and contraception centres. The Margaret Pyke Centre in Camden, for instance, faced a funding cut to its contraceptive services, which means that especially vulnerable women won't have access to emergency contraception. The centre helps women dealing with female genital mutilation and domestic violence, and for some women this is the only time they are in regular contact with healthcare professionals.

I met Dr Jayne Kavanagh, principal clinical teaching fellow at University College London, a clinician at the

Margaret Pyke Centre and the leader of the Save Margaret Pyke campaign. We sat in a huge Victorian wood-panelled boardroom in a basement at University College London, and she talked about the centre where she's worked once a week for over nineteen years with an almost reverent tone.

Margaret Pyke's core service since it was founded in 1969 has been advising and supplying contraception – but, by the nature of the work, it also deals with issues around sexually transmitted infection, sexual abuse and domestic violence. 'It might be some women's first encounter with a healthcare professional – especially for teenagers who may have never seen a doctor or a nurse before. Our role in picking up other things going on in people's lives is very important. I've dealt with women gang-raped in a war zone and discovered past sexual abuse when someone's come for a cervical smear. You can help women to talk about issues they may never have talked about before – and then signpost, if it's appropriate, to psychological services, for instance.'

The centre has been nipped at by cuts almost since it opened. Twenty years ago, the Margaret Pyke Centre ran community clinics in the middle of council estates – for people who don't tend to travel far out of their communities or women whose partners wouldn't let them come to something labelled as a 'sexual health clinic' but would come to something labelled as a 'family planning clinic'. These services were cut some time ago, but things seemed more hopeful in 2012 when the centre moved from its old Charlotte Street building to an impressive new place in King's Cross – 'all state-of-the-art exposed brickwork – it really said to women, "We care about you. We value you,"' says Kavanagh.

Also in 2012, however, the Health and Social Care Act fragmented health commissioning services and gave responsibility for sexual health to local authorities. Although every £1 spent on contraception saves the NHS £11 – meaning by any reckoning the Margaret Pyke Centre's 20,000 consultations a year is good value for money – for cash-strapped councils this budget was a significant new expense. Sexual health accounted for roughly 30 per cent of councils' public health budgets at the time of transfer – and, in July 2015, the government announced a £200 million, or 6.2 per cent, cut to the public health budget. The cut amounted to a total reduction of £800 million over four years.

After the cut was announced, Central and North West London (CNWL) NHS Foundation Trust – which runs the Margaret Pyke Centre on behalf of Camden Council – began looking at ways to reduce costs. The decision-making group was purely managerial – no clinicians involved. In summer 2015, through careful reading of management speak, the staff realised they were planning to shut the centre. 'I wrote to the woman leading the so-called transformation review stating our concerns and asking for representation on the panel,' Kavanagh explains. 'She was very polite and respectful but basically said no. I emailed three times just to be sure that she understood that I was really concerned and that I would take action if my concerns weren't met, and they weren't. So I thought, "What choice do we have? Only people power."'

As Kavanagh's employer was University College London, she felt safe enough to lead the protests. Other full-time staff, already threatened with redundancy, were less confident so she recruited some retired staff members, and together they launched the campaign in October with a series of high-profile media stunts to gain public attention. 'People don't know when cuts are being made, they just know when they've happened,' Kavanagh explains. 'We wanted to let people know while there was still a chance.'

The first stunt was a suffragette protest – former staff in suffragette costumes chained themselves to the railings outside the centre, picking up coverage in local and national press. In December, around fifty teenage school students with fake baby bumps sang rewritten lyrics to Pink Floyd's 'Another Brick in the Wall' outside a full council meeting at Islington Town Hall:

> We all need our contraception
> We all need our birth control
> No unwanted pregnancies in the classroom
> CNWL: leave our clinic alone

Appropriately, the original schoolchildren singing, 'We don't need no education' on the 1979 hit were all students at nearby Islington Green School. The protest was broadcast live on BBC local news and picked up by local TV and press. By the time they launched a fundraiser comedy gig, even Capital FM had Kavanagh in for an interview.

And then, on New Year's Eve, they seemed to get a result. CNWL issued a statement agreeing to a public consultation. Shortly afterwards, the woman leading the consultation took early retirement and a new team arrived who seemed keener to talk. Over the spring they met and agreed to seven principles, including that at least 70 per cent of the existing Margaret Pyke Centre service would be kept in one location, the centre would keep the Margaret Pyke name, any new location would have at least 8–10 clinical rooms dedicated to contraception and women's sexual and reproductive health provision, and the quality of service and training would not suffer.

Finally, as expected, the shiny new centre was closed down and services moved to an existing GUM/HIV clinic in Mortimer Street. Campaigners threatened to march between the two if, as suddenly seemed likely, the name would disappear. In May, the move took place.

Although the campaign kept a large chunk of the centre's services from being cut – and kept the centre's original name, so that local people could send their children to the same place they'd first received advice – Kavanagh feels defeated.

'This tide of underfunding is impossible to stop,' she explains. 'This isn't just us – there's been closures in West London, Northamptonshire, Cheshire, Dorset, Gloucestershire, Berkshire and Bexley. It's going on across the country.' In December 2016, an FOI request from the Advisory Group on Contraception found that 14 per cent of councils had closed at least one site in 2015–16, while another eighteen (13 per cent) said that clinics could be closed in 2016. One and a half million women of reproductive age are affected.

In February 2017, the Margaret Pyke campaign became the Campaign for Contraception. They announced the news in January by floating a giant condom balloon over Trafalgar Square and plan on fresh stunts every bank holiday across the country. 'It's about valuing women isn't it?' says Kavanagh. 'That's the thing – just ordinary women going about their lives. It's about saying, "You're important and we're going to support you in this very important aspect of your life." It's not dramatic. It's not emergency based – but it's very important and it shouldn't be ignored.'

Kavanagh's campaign – planned and led by women – is part of an increasing trend. 'Women have always been at the heart of working-class communities, but what's changed recently is their visibility,' argues Lisa McKenzie, author of *Getting By: Estates, Class and Culture in Austerity Britain.* 'If you look at protests like the Focus E15 Mums who occupied vacant East London flats in 2014 in protest at plans to demolish a housing estate, it's women who are fighting back as activists as well.'

McKenzie grew up in Sutton-in-Ashfield, a mining town, and moved to the St Ann's estate in Nottingham in 1988, a council estate housing 15,000 people who rely upon social housing and public services to – as McKenzie says – 'keep their heads above water'. Via an open-access course, she eventually completed her PhD thesis with an eight-year ethnographic study of the estate. 'In my oral exam, they asked, "Where are the men?"' she recalls. 'I'd spent twenty years on that estate and I didn't know. So I went back and had a look – all the male buildings, the pubs, the working men's clubs, all the male spaces have closed. They now live "Pass By" lives – passing by their mums, their sister, the barbers and the gym. They're transient.'

As shattered post-industrial areas – where the old idea of community was based around the workplace – struggle with the newly fragmented world of work and worklessness, it's small groups of determined women who are holding things together. 'Women hold up far more than half of the sky today,' says Angus McCabe of Birmingham University's

Third Sector Research Centre. 'Men used to come to community organising through trade union activity while in employment. Now the majority of community organisations and grass roots activism is led by women.'

Data on how many women are leading community-level organisations are hard to come by, but figures from the National Council for Voluntary Organisations show that, of the 800,000 people it counts in the voluntary sector, almost two-thirds are women. Wigan-based Barbara Nettleton is one of these. As a child, growing up in post-war Wigan, she helped her mother organise fundraising beetle drives – a common post-war fundraising evening where the game of Beetle, essentially bingo with insect body parts, was played for money – while the men of the community occupied positions and sat on committees at the working men's clubs and local trade unions. 'The community was organised through the working men's clubs – and women weren't even allowed in the tap rooms,' she recalls.

She still lives in the town, up the hill from the site of the infamous tripe shop where George Orwell stayed when he came to research *The Road to Wigan Pier*. The buildings he described are long gone – there's a car park where the tripe shop used to be – but the area is still one of the poorest in Wigan. Now in her sixties, Nettleton runs Sunshine House, a community centre behind Scholes Precinct, a concrete shopping parade teetering on the brink of desolation. The area has changed little over the decades, but now those on the front line between hardship and officialdom are women. 'My whole board, all my senior staff, are women,' she says.

Nettleton set up a residents' association in 1997, after

drugs started flooding the area and one of her neighbours was beaten to death in his house. 'We got together to build a bit of community spirit,' she explains. Ten years ago, just as her husband was diagnosed with terminal cancer, the group expanded into Sunshine House.

It started with art classes. 'When the mines and the steelworks and the mills closed, it took the apprenticeships away,' Nettleton explains. 'If you get kids into art and design, it's a skill they can use.' She also runs a lottery with a bonus ball for police officers, meaning patrol cars often stop by for a ticket, thus raising the police presence in the area. The lottery helps fund a community chest, which gives spot loans with no interest and no fixed repayments to local people struggling with bills or in short-term need.

As the council's care budget was whittled away, Sunshine House launched groups for people with mental health conditions who, thanks to benefit changes, no longer qualified to use day centres. The centre works with the Veterans Council to distribute grants, helps launch micro-enterprises and organises computer training. A café offers hot food at low prices, and the centre is considering digging up its flowerbeds to plant fruit and vegetables for families struggling with sanctions. It is in discussions with the local healthcare professionals on how to help people with eating disorders. 'We're a bit like doctors anyway,' says Nettleton. 'You think of the community as the body, with all the problems and issues of an industrial area. We keep checking the problems and dressing them in different ways.'

The Beveridge Report, unfortunately, has little space for women like Barbara. Beveridge assumed men's responsibilities and claims were defined by their relationship to work, but women were defined primarily by their marital status. Men were the breadwinners and were expected to work full-time to support their dependent wife caring for their children – 'During marriage,' he believed, 'most women will not be gainfully occupied . . . The attitude of the housewife to gainful employment outside the home is not and should not be the same as that of the single woman.' With a whiff of his taste for eugenics, women were encouraged to have children to stop the 'British race' disappearing.

Today, in certain senses, the position is reversed. When it comes to caring for dependents, across the UK, community centres, crisis drop-in projects and GP surgeries are responding to the years of cuts and austerity with a range of improvised and creative strategies to defend their communities. As with Sunshine House, women are taking the lead. In South Wales around thirty years ago there were more Miners' Welfare Institutes than days of the year, according to Andrew Morse of the Coal Industry Social Welfare Organisation. Today there are just thirty-eight. 'Thirty years ago, the boards of trustees of those institutes would be overwhelmingly if not entirely male,' says Morse. 'Today, way more than half our trustees are women.'

In Newcastle, the Citizens Advice Bureau has come a long way from 1939, when the first office opened their doors and 'it was only men who were allowed to give advice', according to Shona Alexander. As CEO of the Newcastle branch, she heads a largely female leadership team, which runs stalls in a local Tesco, pop-up stalls in the community and has started training programmes helping the digitally deprived understand online benefits forms.

In Leicester, Inclusion Healthcare is a GP practice and social enterprise running the city's homeless healthcare founded by CEO Anna Hiley and executive director Jane Gray, whom we met in Chapter 6.

The all-female team knew that in 2016 they'd have to compete for the contract again. 'So we needed to grow, to become more sustainable, so that next time we could compete with the more commercial organisations out there,' she explains. They've taken on contracts for substance misuse services, some within the local prison, as well as the young people's drug team and an asylum seekers' practice originally run by Virgin Healthcare, who recently withdrew from the contract. They've gone from a staff of seven to a staff of forty-two, and the turnover's gone from about £800,000 to £2.4 million over a four-year period. This is all designed to ensure the practice becomes big and robust enough to offer some of the cost efficiencies that a larger organisation might bring.

I first met the Inclusion team in early 2016 and went back at the start of 2017. At that point, the homeless healthcare contract review had been postponed until later in the year, having gone through the entire repitching process in the summer. Hiley was immensely frustrated but grimly determined to carry on.

I found the same resolution in Lesley Hodgson, who runs a community art project in Merthyr Tydfil that manages drop-in advice alongside significant bridge-building between local Welsh residents and the Portuguese and Eastern European workers who have moved here during the last decade. This work is a bid to overcome the source of tension that made Merthyr a UKIP target in recent campaigns.

Merthyr boomed from the late 1700s to the early twentieth century as the main town in the coal-rich Welsh Valleys – for a long time it was the largest town in Wales. As the coal industry declined from the 1930s, government agencies rushed to attract manufacturing industries to the area. Hoover opened a large plant in 1948, employing over 5,000 workers during the 1970s. At one point, Merthyr's nickname was 'Hooverville'. In the 1980s, these manufacturing employers shut down, usually to move production to cheaper countries overseas. These days Merthyr has a population of just 58,000 and has had some of the highest levels of economic inactivity in Britain – in 1997 it had the highest rate of unemployment in the country at 33 per cent.

Merthyr's town centre has wide, open streets and low stone buildings that give it the feel of a Regency market town. Any trace of its industrial past has been scrubbed clean and the buildings painted with bright pastel colours. Focal Point is based out of a former shop on the high street, with its wide display windows filled by leaflets, posters and handbills. When I arrived, Lesley, who looks young for her sixty years with blonde bob-cut hair, was helping someone fill out a job application form. Eventually we sit at a long table covered with example forms for housing benefit or jobs in a variety of languages, with English translations printed alongside.

She was almost Merthyr born and bred, she begins. Technically she was born in Stratford-upon-Avon, 'But I never tell people that . . . My father was doing his national service there in the RAF, then we came back when I was six months old.' Aged seventeen she moved to Ireland with her parents – where her dad worked as a delivery driver for

Coca-Cola and her mum worked as a nurse. They kept themselves to themselves and didn't mix with the locals.

She met and married her husband there – a Geordie – then came back to Merthyr where they had three children and spent a lot of time missing Ireland. 'So we went back and this time I was determined to make sure that we integrated as much as possible,' she recalls. 'My youngest daughter was born there and the kids all learned Irish at school. We had a much happier time there the second time and I am sure that's because we made the effort to kind of get involved as much as possible.' In the end her marriage didn't survive and she came back to Merthyr in 1994 with her four children, working out what to do with her life.

The town that she returned to was changing. When she was a kid she remembered putting clothes out on the line and they'd come in covered in black soot, but the town was cleaning up. She decided to study and went to the nearby University of Glamorgan. 'I was lucky,' she nods. 'I went in the last year they had the grant system and you could be on income support and study so that's how I made it financially.' She blushes. 'And I kind of deejayed. Weddings and birthday parties and things like that. It seems crazy now but that's how I supported us while I was at university.'

Graduating in 2000 with a first-class degree, she started a PhD in civil society post-devolution and worked as a sociology lecturer at Glamorgan, but was getting a little disillusioned with academic life: 'the pressure of writing the same thing in six different ways to get journal articles out', she grimaces. 'I didn't feel as if I was having an impact on the real world, I suppose.'

In 2004, the university set up an education access project called Glamorgan Gates in Merthyr, getting people involved in informal learning using art projects as a route to more formal learning. 'It was engaging young people in, say, music projects and then taking them down to the university to record a CD and have a tour of the university and introduce them to academic life,' she explains. 'Inspiring them or just getting them used to the idea that it was an option.'

At the same time as Gates was starting up, the town was starting to experience a wave of immigration from mainland Europe. In 1999, a meat processing plant opened up on the Penygarnddu Industrial Estate. It's a huge plant – with the capacity to slaughter and de-bone 2,400 cattle and 24,000 lamb per week, as well as packing 1,300 tonnes per week for retail. The original founders, a Cornish company called St Merryn, had been enticed by land and £15 million from the Welsh Office and the Welsh Development Agency to bring sorely needed jobs to the area.

St Merryn was at the heart of a government strategy to create a regional manufacturing sector. Announcing the factory's launch at a press conference in Merthyr in January 1997, Secretary of State for Wales William Hague boasted that the factory would create 'seven hundred well-paid jobs, here in Merthyr – exactly the right sort of jobs, in exactly the right place'.

Within a couple of years of opening, St Merryn began to import workers from Portugal through an employment agency called Atlanco. By 2005, about a hundred of St Merryn's workforce of 900 were Portuguese. After the A8 Eastern European nations joined the EU in 2004, St Merryn began recruiting from Poland, replacing Atlanco with Staffline – a British agency based in Nottingham that specialises in recruiting food industry workers across Europe and turned over £1 billion in 2017. A BBC investigation in 2006 found Polish meat processing plant workers recruited by Staffline were living thirteen to a house and earning much less than they'd been promised out in Krakow. By 2008, over 61 per cent of the factory's workforce were migrants.

To understand why these changes happened, Stuart Tannock – then a researcher at Cardiff University, now at University College London – interviewed locals and migrants and tried to interview St Merryn's management, who declined his invitation. His resulting paper, 'Bad Attitude? Migrant Workers, Meat Processing Work and the Local Unemployed in a Peripheral Region of the UK', is a detailed blow-by-blow account of a story currently playing out across post-industrial Britain.

In 2000, the company told a Welsh government research team that it was unable to find local workers with the skills it needed in Merthyr. These necessary skills included 'an awareness of basic food hygiene . . . commitment, ambition, social skills, common sense, and a responsible attitude'. Tabloids picked this up and all but the *Daily Mirror* ran stories on St Merryn, calling Merthyr 'the sicknote capital of the UK' and claiming St Merryn was 'forced to fly in workers' from Portugal and Poland because Merthyr locals, living in a 'benefits comfort zone', would 'rather go on the sick . . . than take a low-paid job'.

One local employee who had been with the company since it arrived and still worked there told Tannock a different story: 'Starting off, St Merryn were bastards. There's no other word for them. The manager would say . . . he wouldn't say it nice . . . "Fucking get over there now and pack them fucking steaks now, you little bastard." "Whoa!

Hang about mate, who the fuck do you think you're talking to here?" "You, if you don't fucking like it, there's the door, make your fucking choice now." . . . Some people didn't like that and they went. If they had treated the staff differently, we'd probably still be all Welsh over there, but they came here with bullyboy antics . . . "Sack you? No problem, there's another fucking twenty behind you." . . . They get somebody else in. "Fuck off, there's another nineteen behind you, that's no problem." All of a sudden, "Fuck off. Oh, um, we haven't got anyone else behind him anymore. What are we going to do now? I tell you what, we'll get Portuguese in here."

Tannock found past and present workers, local and migrant, agreed. Migrant workers hated St Merryn and many of them went home. Others – those that could speak English – found other jobs in the area. So when it comes to lazy Merthyr, who are we to believe? The children of people who worked underground in coalmines for 200 years shovelling rock then helped build a vast Hoover plant? The great grandchildren of the Merthyr men Thomas Carlyle described as the hardest working and fiercest he had ever seen? Or a company that took £15 million in a sweetheart deal to open in an area with the highest unemployment in the country? Who was trying to take advantage of whom?

By 2005 the first-wave migrant population was large enough, although still tiny in terms of Merthyr's overall population, that someone set up a little Portuguese coffee shop called Serrano's just opposite the library. Very soon there were rumours going around that locals not only struggled to get work in the factory but they couldn't get served in the Portuguese coffee shop because they were British. 'So

I went there, to the coffee shop, and literally sat in the window for a year, every Monday morning because people would know me and if somebody walked past that I happened to know, I'd run out and say, come on in, come on in,' Leslie explains. 'And then I thought, do you know, while we're sat here, I could be developing some sort of project around art.'

She contacted a local photographer whose work involved giving disposable cameras to people to document their lives. They sat in the coffee shop together learning a little Portuguese and making friends 'and then we gave people – local and Portuguese – cameras and told them to just take photographs of whatever they liked and always use the flash, even on the brightest of days', she explains. 'We chose the best photographs and had a little display up in the coffee shop – but people kept coming up to us until we had a hundred participants over a year long and we had displays throughout town, then an exhibition of large prints that toured Cardiff and North Wales. We even made postcards. Then people began to bring photographs from their past life. We started recording their stories and everybody was bringing food to the sessions so we developed cookery books.'

Eventually she set up a drop-in session at the Gates project helping the new workers with rent and employment issues, and running English classes – 'anything that would support new people coming to Merthyr Tydfil', she smiles. As the profile of the newcomers changed, Gates started working with Poles, Romanians and Bulgarians, and Lesley realised this was where her heart was. 'I'd moved away and lived elsewhere in Ireland and Newcastle – which I loved, but Merthyr was where I came back to and I've always thought it's a very welcoming place,' she explains. 'I don't understand this attitude to migrant workers – which is such a horrible word. We call them newly arrived communities.'

Money was trickling into the town. The Welsh government gave St Merryn £1.2 million in 2010, defence contractor General Dynamics opened a new factory to build the Ajax armoured vehicle, and Cornish department store Trago Mills announced plans to build a store. Lesley won funding from the Big Lottery to start Focal Point – a support charity that still has culture and cultural exchange at its core. There's a Polish and Welsh night, a multicultural Christmas event and a summer Global Village Festival that attracts around 5,000 people. There's also a drop-in centre with Portuguese and Polish translators helping people with everything from liaising with the council to filling in job application forms.

For a while Lesley felt things were working out. 'Initially around 2004–5 there had been this little peak and then everything seemed to die down – you're always going to get some people who don't like newcomers but in the main everything was fine,' she explains. Then UKIP targeted Merthyr Tydfil in the 2015 election. They opened a little office opposite an Indian restaurant and next door to a Tunisian coffee shop, with a Portuguese café and a Polish hairdresser and Focal Point all nearby. Newly arrived community members started feeling a negative backlash. 'UKIP was peddling false rumours – they're actually on film outside the Polish supermarket saying – "I've heard you can't go in there if you're a Welsh person,"' Lesley recalls. 'I thought we'd got over that back in 2004–5 and here it was again ten years later rearing its head – and it's patently not true.'

UKIP left after the election but returned during the EU referendum, targeting solid Labour-voting areas like the

Gurnos estate, a sprawling 1950s development with high unemployment. 'We had people saying things like, yeah, my shed's been broken in seven times, we've got a lot of Polish people living in our street,' Lesley shakes her head. 'You'd ask, "Are you saying it was a Polish person that did that?" They'd reply, "Oh, no, I'm not saying that, but you know . . ." And once there's a correlation in people's minds they begin to think it's a causal effect when it's not.'

Merthyr voted leave by 56 per cent. Lesley heard stories from her clients of people going into work the day after the referendum and reaching across a Portuguese or Polish worker to congratulate their Welsh colleague, saying – 'we did it!' 'There was one estate where there was a big party the Friday night after the referendum and a Polish lady was told, "It's a Brexit party, you're not welcome,"' Lesley recalls. 'The next day her children went out to play and the other children said, "We're not allowed to play with you anymore because you're going to go back to Poland." You had people saying things like, "Oh, you'll have to pack your bags," but saying it with a smile and a laugh. They call it celebratory racism – like, if you laugh you can say – "I was joking!" But it has a huge impact on people. In the end that Polish family did go back – they were made to feel so uncomfortable and the police did nothing to help so they left.'

But she also started getting mostly anonymous letters through the door from locals aimed at migrant workers saying, 'We can't believe it and we're really sorry, we don't want you to go.' One said, 'I've never spoken to a Polish person but I really am glad you're here because you've built up our economy.' She started pinning the letters to the wall, then – at 2016's Global Village Festival – asked locals to add to them.

The 'welcome messages' now cover almost half of one wall, arranged so that they appear to be tumbling down like a swiftly flowing river. As people came in to add new messages, she started recruiting them for a mixed nations football team – five different national backgrounds all on the same side. In September, the Merthyr Migrant team played local side Quar Park Rangers in front of hundreds of spectators and the Wales manager Chris Coleman.

Then, in November 2016, St Merryn's owners – 2 Sisters Food Group – announced it was moving the retail packing operation back to St Merryn's Cornish base. Out of a total staff of 1,000, 350 were likely to be made redundant. Tension has built over which nationalities will lose the jobs. 'The hardest hit are those people who came with an agency which did all the paperwork for them and they've stayed in the factory the whole time so they have enough English to get by in work but they don't have the English to go for interviews,' she explains. 'We've had lots of families settle – the children are going to schools here.'

Despite this, Lesley is optimistic about the future, and about her community. 'I've been somebody who would always look for consensus in the past but now I just think we can't let this slip by,' she explains. 'I see it from both sides, you know. Underneath everything there's this hidden poverty. I work with the Citizens Advice Bureau and there's always a queue of people on a Thursday morning looking for debt advice. But we've got great things happening in and around Merthyr – I've always seen it as a place of safety. There's so much potential. We just need to do something about it.'

11

Courage, Faith and Unity

The social surveys made by impartial investigators of living conditions in some of the main industrial centres of Britain have been used earlier in this Report to supply a diagnosis of want. They can be used also to show that the total resources of the community were sufficient to make want needless.

The plan for social security in this report is submitted by one who believes that in this supreme crisis the British people will not be found wanting, of courage and faith and national unity, of material and spiritual power to play their part in achieving both social security and the victory of justice among nations upon which security depends.

Sir William Beveridge, *Social Insurance and Allied Services Report*

Folkestone's gold rush began on 28 August 2016, when contractors employed by German artist Michael Sailstorfer buried thirty gold bars worth a total of £10,000 in a strip of beach nestling just inside the tiny harbour. Some were buried six metres deep using heavy machinery. Others were just a few centimetres below the surface. He called the work 'Folkestone Digs'.

The news came at a press conference announcing the third Folkestone Triennial – the town's three-month arts festival featuring twenty-five commissioned new works. 'They showed us the first twenty-four works then told us about the twenty-fifth,' explains Dean Kilpatrick, reporter on the *Folkestone Herald*. 'There were a couple of art critics down from the national broadsheets and they went crazy for the story. It blew up from there.'

ITV Breakfast, *BBC News* – even Chinese state television – broadcast live from the town. Folkestone's Creative Foundation, which runs the Triennial, counted 119 articles in regional, national and international media, fourteen items on radio and television, and more than 200 online articles attracting over 1.6 billion hits. Sales of digging tools including trowels, shovels and spades increased by almost 500 per cent at the local B&Q store.

For some, however, the story was severely underreported. 'The parishes around the harbour have been very badly affected over the past twenty years,' according to the Reverend David Adlington, the priest in charge of St Peter's church, which perches on the hill above Folkestone Harbour. 'I think it's in questionable taste at the very least to bury gold under the noses of the poor as an art stunt. But the papers and the TV didn't really look at that – they just treated the story as a bit of silly season fun.'

The three wards that border Folkestone harbour – Folkestone East, Folkestone Harbour and Folkestone Harvey Central – are among the poorest in Kent. Adlington's parish, which roughly covers Folkestone Harbour Ward, has one-third of its children and one in five working adults living in poverty.

In both Folkestone Harbour and Folkestone Harvey Central, around 10 per cent of the population are unemployed and the three wards are at the bottom of the life expectancy rates in Shepway. Men in Folkestone Harbour have a life expectancy of seventy-three years, six years lower than the national average and seven years lower than nearby Folkestone Park. Over the past ten years, hospital admissions for drinking and drug-taking in the whole of Shepway have been on an upward trend.

Walking the short, sandy beach under the shadow of the harbour wall in the weeks after the gold was first buried, I found the vast majority of diggers were unemployed or low waged. In September I met Michelle Moorin and Anthony Bevan digging with spades, hands and bits of wood. Michelle had been unemployed for just under a year after the shop she worked in closed. She moved to Folkestone from Yorkshire when she was eight and still remembers looking along the beach at the Rotunda, the sprawling amusement park dismantled in 2003. 'I couldn't believe all the lights and the noise,' she beams. 'It was like arriving somewhere magical. In my teens it was brilliant – you could go out every night. There was always something going on. Now everything's just empty and wrecked.' She returned to her digging cheerfully, saying someone found a bar nearby earlier that day so she figured she was working a lucky spot.

In October I met John Knott working the beach with a metal detector. He'd worked at HMV until the chain collapsed in 2013, and bought the metal detector shortly after. He spends his time prospecting for discarded metal and had been to the beach a few times. 'I've found some coins and a couple of pieces of jewellery so far, but no bullion,' he explained. 'I saw a couple find a piece yesterday – watched them dig it up – and they just hustled off without saying a word to anyone.'

Three weeks later Becky Rachman was working the same patch as Michelle. She'd read Facebook stories that four bars had been found and decided to give it a try. 'I've just been made redundant,' she explained. 'I used to work in publishing but that's over now, so I'm a gold digger.' She laughed. 'I mean it's better than sitting around watching telly.'

'There are fewer people on colder days – but the coldest day I went there was in February and there was still one guy digging away . . . The digging has never really stopped,' explains Kilpatrick. 'There were even people there on Christmas day.' Sailstorfer's artwork has become a documentary of despair: a performance of Folkestone's unemployed digging. The tragedy is the Triennial was supposed to help regenerate a struggling town, not mock its inhabitants.

The Triennial is funded by local boy made good Roger de Haan, who sold his Folkestone-based travel company SAGA Holidays for £1.4 billion in 2004. He decided to invest much of the money into the town, which was clearly in dire need. Ferries to Boulogne, France, used to operate out of the harbour and the town was built and flourished on the tourist and fishing trades. Tontin Street – now a seedy area with a reputation for drug dealing – used to boast glamorous boutiques and the Orient Express ran through on its way to Paris. When the Channel Tunnel opened in 1994, however, the slow decline faced by all British seaside towns since the 1960s rapidly accelerated.

In the years before the tunnel opened, Folkestone's two remaining ferries – the *Hengist* and the *Horsa* – each employed a crew of fifty-six to one hundred according to season. In the 1970s the port handled around 75,000 passengers, 4,000 cars, fifty coaches and 400 freight vehicles per month. After the tunnel opened, a high-speed Seacat Folkestone–Boulogne service struggled on until September 2000. The harbour closed the following year and the railway line, which still carried Orient Express day trips, closed in 2009.

'Folkestone has been left behind,' argues Richard Bellamy, manager of the Rainbow Centre, Folkestone's church-funded homeless charity. 'There's been a tremendous lack of investment; it's very hard to gain employment – and that's key to getting people to help themselves out of homelessness.' Perched above a café on Sandgate Street, the centre offers help – from washing and drying facilities through help with official forms to advice on accommodation and supplies of emergency food every weekday morning. Between 2012 and 2013 the rise in attendance was 67 per cent. From 2013 to 2014 it rose by 27 per cent to some 600 people.

'We've also seen greater prejudice towards our clients, I think,' continues Bellamy. 'People think of folk here as being dependent – but the vast majority have lived in the world of work, want work and want the dignity that work brings. Employment's key. If there's work to be done, people generally want to do that. If there isn't the work, people just spiral down and feel less hopeful about the future. Sanctions, whatever their intention, make that harder and make people more dependent on hand-outs and food banks for survival. No one wants to be saved by gold buried in the sand. The vast majority don't want quick fixes, they want to live ordinary life well and it should humble all of us.'

De Haan's plan placed creativity, art and culture at the heart of regeneration. 'This part of the harbour was never used for leisure purposes – and Michael Sailstorfer's artwork has changed that,' Lewis Biggs, curator of Folkestone's Triennial argued. 'It is now a leisure beach used by people for enjoying the sun and digging. This is symptomatic of the economy of Folkestone, because the leisure industry has to come in and pick up some pieces. If the harbour has a future it is because of the leisure industry and this artwork has expressed that change in a way that people can understand.' De Haan himself and Michael Sailstorfer refused to be interviewed.

In many ways, the dream of regeneration in Folkestone is a dry run for the dream of a post-industrial UK. It involved a high-powered mix of billionaires, cultural industries and high-speed rail networks. It is a small-scale simulacrum of the government's current plans for redeveloping the north of the country. HS1 – the country's first high-speed rail link between St Pancras and the south coast – began a full time-table of high-speed service in December 2009, with limited services running from that summer. As a consequence de Haan's redevelopment should be flushing the town with cash. The Creative Quarter should be packed with shops and tourists. The economy should be bubbling. 'In fact, the whole of east Kent has slightly underperformed against the rest of the southeast since HS1 opened,' says Dr Richard Wellings, head of transport at the Institute for Economic Affairs. 'The ticket prices are sold at a premium – making it too expensive for commuters and families looking for a seaside day out. It's like Doncaster – which has had high-speed rail for thirty years and is still one of the most deprived parts of the country.'

'The whole development makes no sense,' says Terry Noakes, secretary of the Folkestone Fisherman's Association, which represents the remaining trawlers in town. 'There's not a fisherman's museum, a sea life centre, amusements – there's nothing, is there? He should dredge the harbour, build a marina – not build expensive fish restaurants and paint the high street.'

Even the art world is dubious. J. J. Charlesworth is critic and associate editor of the London-based international art magazine *ArtReview*. He moved to Folkestone six years ago and is 'very pessimistic' about the regeneration possibilities of events like the Triennial. 'I don't really think that art can save us from poverty at all,' he explained. 'I don't see the Triennial having any immediate effect in Folkestone – except possibly to raise shop rents. There are a lot of empty shops in town now. It is too easy to parachute a biennial or a triennial into a community. Often they only benefit investors and property developers and don't benefit local people.'

Back on the beach I met Billy. He's got a low, halting voice with the gravelly rasp of a cockney accent. He used to be a pub landlord, running pubs along the Old Kent Road and the Walworth Road, before taking on the Baring Hall Hotel in Grove Park for Punch Taverns in 2004. He moved in with his girlfriend and it went well for a while. The company spent £170,000 doing the place up in keeping with its traditional old-pub look. Then local drug dealers offered him £4,000 to deal from the pub. He refused and a row broke out

– he had a good rapport with people from the nearby Downham Estate and a few of them jumped in to help, but it escalated and he was stabbed. After that, things went downhill. He was threatened and attacked until one night in August 2009 the pub was firebombed. Fire crews took eight hours to bring the flames under control.

He took a bar job in nearby Bromley. Then his girlfriend left after the trouble put strain on their relationship, and his mum died very shortly after. One day he took a train to Romney Marsh, found a pub and started drinking. He woke up in the morning with no memory. He spent six months living on Romney Sands beach until, during the bad snow in the winter of 2010, a woman from Folkestone's Porchlight charity came out to help him. She took him to hospital where doctors diagnosed a nervous breakdown brought on by the stabbing, the firebombing, the relationship breaking down and his mum dying.

It took him a full year to get his faculties back. He used to stand outside shops and wait for people to open the door because he wasn't sure what to do. His memory was coming back in flashes, but he'd do daft stuff like putting custard and baked beans in a pan together. He stayed in local churches over the winter then moved down the beach to the Warren, a little shantytown community with handmade shacks where four or five outsleepers lived. He did memory courses with Mind – writing everything down. He even had his own name written down in a little book.

In 2011 he was stabbed again – down by the harbour the night before his birthday. Four men wanted his rucksack and in the scuffle he was stabbed in the back and arm, which required forty-eight stitches. He rolls up his sleeve to show me the mark – a messy slash of white scar tissue. 'Lucky it happened to me rather than a couple, because someone could have got hurt really badly,' he says mildly.

After that, Porchlight helped find him a flat, although a couple of months ago he was given an eviction notice. The landlord had sold the building because regeneration is driving up house prices and being a social landlord wasn't paying. 'Being on sickness benefit I'm only entitled to £375 a month and most of the market rents are between £400 and £500,' he explains. He has two months to get out and he's worried his fourteen-year-old daughter, Sofia, will stop visiting him. She'd not come down while he was at the Warren but she'd liked the flat. 'So this Christmas I might be in a shelter and she won't like that.'

He still suffers from voices in his head: 'I'm medicated for it. I've got a psychiatrist in town, Dr Barron. Sometimes I have good stages, sometimes I have bad stages. I wish I could get rid of it, I wish I could not stay up two or three nights without sleep. I wouldn't like to have a partner now, it's better I'm alone. It's quite hard when you're a homeless fella. I've never had a bad episode while someone was there but you never know.'

He tries to get out and about as much as he can: 'I've always been quite a fit person, so I go to the gym, I go to the library . . . I'm not a person that just likes to sit indoors, I'm not an internet person. I do talk to my daughter on Facebook but that's it.' He looks out over the beach. 'I come down and watch people digging – and sometimes at low tide I have a look to see if the sand's been washed away and there's gold,' he says quietly. 'But there never is.'

~

Folkestone is an object lesson in the wrong way to try and save broken communities. Historically there has been a set of oppositional ideas, from the luddites to the chartists to the anarchists to the Kibbo Kift to old-school socialists, which gave people the option not just of ideas about changing their situation but also a chance to take pride in their identity. Today, under neoliberalism's heavy cloak of uniformity, those ideas have all but disappeared.

Across the country, however, I found inspiring examples and solutions from people doing their best to live an ordinary life well. These are individual stories rather than a grand ideological manifesto or set of solutions – but, taken together, they offer a sense of hope and suggest a different way of thinking.

Some of these ideas – from the likes of Shelter and soldier's charity Veteran's Aid – are simple but ambitious. Shelter's John Bibby argues that there's a very straightforward way to fund the building of affordable homes to make renting fit for purpose. 'We think the way the garden cities and the new towns were developed still has potential,' he explains. 'In an area where you could build housing, the council or the developer could purchase that land at its existing land value then put in a planning application for development of homes. Then, they could reinvest the resulting uplift in land value back into affordable homes.'

What's happening now in the planning system, he argues, is developers using planning on appeal to overturn council refusal to allow them to build. As a result, all land is potentially house-building land. 'We need to formalise land use so speculative developers can't just win on appeal,' he argues. 'We should be able to say – this land is agriculture, this is housing and this is housing that the council will buy. That's how we can plan communities that are genuinely mixed with good infrastructure and high design standards. People do want to see new homes built but when they're put up they aren't affordable enough, they've got poor infrastructure, it's tricky getting a GP or finding schools and houses are low quality and not in keeping with the area. We're not taking enough advantage of the potential wrapped up in the value of the land which could make affordable, tasteful homes.'

Over at Veteran's Aid, they've developed a welfare to well-being programme to engage with the root issues of homelessness in ex-soldiers – providing accommodation while also arranging training courses and counselling, or helping deal with alcohol abuse. Hugh Milroy, Veteran's Aid's chief executive, calls it proactive intervention, coupled with long-term commitment and support.

He cites two examples. The first: a young ex-infantry soldier called Dan who came out of the army and struggled to find his feet. 'Poverty and mental health, that's the real issue – poverty and mental health go together and always have done,' says Milroy. 'People look for excuses – GPs treating someone think, "Oh, you were in the army, you must have PTSD." Ten minutes later you're out of the door and on pills that you maybe don't need. So we got Dan off the street into a hotel, gave him money to buy new clothes – we immediately trust people and it's almost always justified.'

To bring down Dan's restless energy, they signed him up to a twenty-four-hour gym – then went through some tests and found his reading age was pretty low. 'We said, "Have you ever thought about being a scaffolder?" He thought that was a good idea. We put him on a course and he's now working. All in, it cost us £1,800 to transform his life. We got him a flat, we put him back. It is not just a hand-out, and it's hugely applicable across society. New clothes, a roof, dealing with issues and then reinvesting in the person and putting them back.'

Elsewhere – as in Northern Ireland and Shirebrook – the solutions were complex and time-consuming, but came from the ground up and, with patience, worked out.

On the last warm day of 2016, I went to Brookeborough in County Fermanagh. I watched a gang of boys kick a football casually around the playground at St Mary's Primary School. Dotted in small groups around them, girls jumped rope and clapped out complicated pat-a-cakes. It was about as ordinary a scene as you'd expect in any school across the country. The only slight anomaly – half the kids were wearing the dark blue jumpers of St Mary's and half had the green jumpers of nearby Brookeborough Primary, just half a mile away down the hill. And in Northern Ireland, that makes all the difference in the world.

St Mary's is a Catholic school, Brookeborough is Protestant, and the small town itself nestles on the edge of southeast Fermanagh – very close to the border with the Irish Republic. During the Troubles – as a border county and a strong Republican area – IRA groups made incursions across the border from the south while British army patrols and checkpoints were regular, heavy and sometimes trigger happy.

As a result, Fermanagh's county town, Enniskillen, saw at least one violent death a year across the 1980s, from the British army shooting a young woman in 1981 to twelve civilians killed by an IRA bomb detonated beside the town war memorial during a Remembrance Day parade in November 1987. It's the county that elected Bobby Sands MP at the height of his hunger strike. The idea that Catholic and Protestant pupils might kick a football around in break time between lessons where they shared a teacher would have been inconceivable ten years ago.

Talking to Ben Foster and Andrew Armstrong, both ten, from Brookeborough and Sean McDermott and Owen Egan, both seven, from St Mary's, the idea that they'd hate each other is equally inconceivable. 'I've got a lot of friends at St Mary's,' Foster said with a shrug. 'I always can't wait for shared education day.'

Shared education is the official name for St Mary's and Brookeborough's collaboration. It's a simple but radical idea in community cohesion. If children from both sides of divided communities came together at school from an early age, it would foster trust. The idea started here, in County Fermanagh, in the cramped office of one man, Lauri McCusker, but has since spread around the world, with UNICEF rolling it out in Macedonia followed by schools in Israel and Palestine, Mexico, Los Angeles and Cyprus.

For McCusker, the forty-something director of local cross-community charity the Fermanagh Community Trust, his greatest satisfaction came in May 2016 when the Shared Education Act received royal assent and his early hunch became official education policy in Northern Ireland. It's an almost Hollywood story: how a handful of people who didn't come from an education background devised and implemented a solution that could work as effectively in Birmingham faith schools or Cypriot Greek and Turkish

schools. Shared education, says McCusker, is about breaking down barriers, however old they are.

'With all the tension, killings, mistrust and fear, Protestants
and Catholics had – and to some extent still have – developed separate worlds,' he explains as we walk down the leafy
hill from St Mary's to Brookeborough Primary. 'You could
live five doors down but you don't engage. In Belfast there
are peace walls. In Fermanagh there are glass walls. You
can't see them, but they are there. And it starts young because
there's almost two education systems in Northern Ireland –
95 per cent of kids go to either a Catholic or a Protestant
school and the schools work in parallel universes.'

McCusker grew up in Enniskillen in the largely Catholic
Cornagrade estate in the 1970s and 1980s. He remembers
baked bean tins popping when a bomb blew out the windows
of his local shop. He remembers walking home from the pub
and cars pulling up close behind him, driving slowly, almost
touching the back of his legs. He remembers waking up in
bed on 8 November 1987 and hearing the enormous blast of
the Remembrance Day bomb. That evening he went to work
his shift at a local petrol station right next to the Enniskillen
police headquarters. The world's media was camped outside
and word gradually filtered through that a guy he knew, who
worked for the same petrol station, had been caught in the
blast.

'We were killing one another,' he says simply. 'I had to
run for my life several times. I came out of a disco once and
the IRA opened fire on the police officers standing next to
me . . . We were doing awful things to one another as a society and a community. There had been so many years of
violence, intimidations – so many people had been involved

and affected by one side or another. By the end of the 1980s, with unemployment so bad, people were just getting out.'

He joined them, moving to Coventry for a degree in economic development and planning. He worked in warehouses in Coventry and London, packing crates for Toys R Us. He travelled, spending six months in southern California working as a gardener and eventually applied for his green card. He was home in Enniskillen getting ready to move out to the USA for good, just saving a bit of money and getting things in order before starting work in Boston, when he saw a job advertised as economic development officer at the local council. 'I was almost gone,' he says, with a faint trace of longing for things unseen in his voice. 'But I couldn't. It was 1994. The peace process was under way. It was a chance to actually do something.'

So he stayed and worked for the council, then a group of housing associations, until the job came up at the Fermanagh Community Trust, a cross-community body funding anything from wind farms to new equipment for sports clubs in the name of growth and cohesion. McCusker joined in 1998 and started running shared pre-schooling, offering mixed nursery places to both communities.

It worked – slowly – until the Labour government introduced free preschool education for all three- and four-year-olds, making the Trust's provision irrelevant overnight. McCusker began looking into primary schools. Ironically, it was Fermanagh's poverty that offered him the solution.

'Fermanagh is a very big, very rural county with small rural primary schools, usually lacking resources,' he explains. 'They've got low pupil numbers and they're usually just down the road from a school from the other community that has the same issues.' The Trust offered to fund specialist teachers – in music or languages – and extra resources for the small, rural primary schools on one condition: to access the teacher or resource, a Catholic school had to share it with a Protestant school and vice versa.

Around this time, one of the Trust's big funders, Atlantic Philanthropies, set up in 1982 by Irish-American business-man Chuck Feeney, was looking for a new direction. Feeney, whose grandmother came from Fermanagh, had been donat-ing heavily to social and public policy schemes to help the peace process. In education, Atlantic had been providing grants to so-called integrated education. This aimed to build specific integrated schools in the hope that both communi-ties would be equally represented. For a few years at the start of the century, Atlantic's Northern Ireland country director, Padraic Quirk, had become increasingly frustrated at the slow rate of growth of integrated schemes. 'In 2004, we decided – let's be a bit more ambitious,' Quirk explains over the phone from Belfast, where he now runs the cross-community Social Change Initiative. 'We wanted to extend our funding to reach the 93 per cent of Northern Ireland pupils who weren't in integrated schools.'

Working with Queen's University, Belfast, Atlantic began developing the philosophy of shared rather than integrated education. 'The beauty of shared education is that it doesn't force kids into integrated schools where their parents worry they'll lose their identity,' explains Professor Joanne Hughes at Queen's University. 'Other short-term initiatives had failed for that reason – it was about community cohesion first and education second. Shared education had to offer more than that – it had to offer a practical benefit for parents, teachers and students with the additional effect of bringing the community together.'

Looking for areas to run trial programmes, Quirk arrived in Fermanagh very quickly. 'Fermanagh people are very precious about the county – if you can get that county to collectively say shared education is for us, we hoped, it could have an effect across all six counties,' Quirk explains. 'And whenever you said you wanted something to be done in Fermanagh, Lauri McCusker's name comes to the top. He somehow knows everybody.'

When you first meet McCusker, this reputation isn't obvious. Indeed, it's tempting to think he's shy. He's a little rumpled and friendly but reserved, sometimes watching you carefully before he replies. Perhaps, you think, he's a little awkward around people. One evening, however, we went out to a local restaurant in the back room of an Enniskillen pub – draped in *Game of Thrones* memorabilia – and it rapidly became clear he knew everyone in the room. Like Frank Sinatra visiting a pasta place in Little Italy, people came up to say hello as if they were literally paying their respects. The restaurant owner wandered through asking if anyone had a white BMW parked outside. He turned to McCusker, who spread out his hands in mock surprise. 'You think?' The landlord laughed. 'Just askin' Lauri – you might have won the lottery.'

Atlantic didn't quite give McCusker a lottery win, but they backed his shared education experiments with £1.7 million, across secondary as well as primary schools. McCusker toured the county, trying to convince parents, teacher and governors. Sometimes the reception was ferociously hostile: he'd stand in front of a tableful of screaming governors for hours before getting chucked out on his ear. But sometimes, schools seemed to have been waiting for him for years.

In Brookeborough, for instance, the two school principals had been trying on and off since the 1970s to arrange a cross-community initiative. Sometimes it was as simple as sharing a bus to swimming lessons. 'There was a certain amount of mixing on the trips,' Brookeborough's principal, Hazel Gardiner, recalls. 'But they tended to get on the bus and sit on their own side – or have Catholics at the front and Protestants at the back. That type of thing.'

The Brookeborough schools were among the first to sign up, and took part in early trials in 2007–8. The benefits to parents were obvious, explains St Mary's principal, Dermot Finlay. Brookeborough currently has seventy-one pupils, and St Mary's just fifty-seven. The threat of closure for both has loomed for years. 'Sharing makes you stronger,' Finlay shrugs. By 2011, there were 3,000 pupils from fifty schools across Fermanagh regularly sharing classrooms and teachers with kids from the other side.

The effect on community tensions has been dramatic. In nearby Newtownbutler, the paramilitary truce in 1994 seemed to spur sectarian street violence, especially during the marching season, where every summer Protestant Orange Orders celebrate historic victories over Catholics. In 1997 the army had to deploy twelve armoured cars in Newtonbutler to help police separate Orange Order members and Republican protestors as rioting spread across the province. The local Orange Lodge suffered smoke damage when a blazing tyre was placed against the wall as recently as 2009. From 2010, however, protests have dwindled. 2015's parades saw fewer than ten Republican protestors on the street, while a loyalist flute band had been invited to play at the Newtownbutler Fleadh a few weeks earlier.

'It's very difficult to directly measure cause and effect – but in Newtownbutler republicanism and loyalism would stand up to each other there every year,' McCusker explains. 'It was a challenge. But over recent years, you've seen the kids from both communities coming together and parents sharing the same school playground – it's very hard to stand on the opposite side of the street screaming at each other if you'll be picking your kids up from the same school gate next week.'

Hughes, Quirk and a group of local Fermanagh politicians agreed, and took McCusker's informal arrangements to then education minister John O'Dowd in 2010. In 2012, O'Dowd appointed an advisory group that reported the following year. Policy proposals followed and, in May 2016, the Shared Education Act received royal assent, making it official government policy across the region. 'Shared education has obvious social and economic benefits but most importantly, there is demonstrable evidence to suggest that it improves educational opportunities and outcomes for our children,' O'Dowd's successor as minister of education, Peter Weir, argues. He sees benefits in all areas where communities are divided or faith schools cause tension. 'I hope schools in the mainland UK and further afield, can see the benefits of sharing,' he adds.

The idea is now spreading internationally. In 2010, UNICEF Macedonia sent policymakers and government officials to Northern Ireland for briefings, workshops and training. The Fermanagh model is now rolling out there.

Since then, charter schools in Los Angeles, teachers and officials from Jerusalem and schools in South Africa have all
asked for help. In January this year, McCusker and his team
sent a video presentation to a conference in Cyprus, where
shared schools may be set up in the buffer zone between
Turkish and Greek Cypriots, although the broad Fermanagh
accent meant the video had to be subtitled in English.

But McCusker isn't interested in some lucrative shared
education consulting role. He remains at the Fermanagh
Community Trust, working on renewable energy plans for
the community. The spread of the idea, he shrugs, is great,
'but the moment for me was here, in Brookeborough last
year when St Mary's and Brookeborough Primary started
talking about a shared campus arrangement – where the two
schools would share the same piece of land and kids would
rub shoulders every day. We were worried that this might be
a step too far so we gathered all the parents together in a
hotel ballroom and explained the plans, then waited. One by
one, the parents stood up and it became clear that they backed
the scheme unanimously. At that point I thought – wow.
We've done it. This is really happening.'

Over in Shirebrook, Sports Direct's Derbyshire base, a
group of local union activists are taking on the agency/zero
hours culture with an entirely new approach to organising:
through protest, political lobbying, pressure on investors,
shaming in the media and teaching English as a second
language.

Shirebrook Miners Welfare Centre is an imposing red-
brick building, two storeys high with a low extension poking
out of the side. For years it's been at the heart of the

community, even through the rough years of the miners strike in 1984–5. Although Shirebrook miners mostly walked out, a significant number carried on working, leading to ugly scenes across the town as police escorted the working miners into the pit. One man I spoke to whose dad kept working was regularly packed into metal bins and thrown down the hill. When he complained to his pro-strike granddad on his mother's side he was told, 'Good. You deserve it. Your dad's a scab.'

Shirebrook is divided today. Fights regularly break out between locals and the Eastern European workers at the Sports Direct warehouse. On the freezing February night I was there, the Welfare Centre was hosting a celebration evening organised by Unite. It was a social gathering for the Sports Direct workers who'd been studying English on the union's free courses and an attempt to bring communities together.

Inside it was a little like a wedding, with children running skidding across the dance floor on their knees and a long buffet table stacked with traditional British buffet food, and traditional Polish food – pickled carrots and hunters stew. There were three generations ambling amiably around, having a bit of a dance and a bit to eat and grumbling that there wasn't enough vodka. The dance floor was packed most of the night, with people starting up conga lines when the DJ played a particularly noisy techno track.

It's the end result of a process that began in 2013 when the union set up Unite Community, opening up union member-ship to people not in paid work. 'Historically, unions have left communities at the same time as employers have deserted them,' Stephen Turner, Unite's assistant general secretary explained when we met in his London office. 'A big workplace withdraws from the community, it goes and sets itself up off the M6 or something because it's closer to transport links and the union went with it. We made a conscious decision that we were going to get back into our heartland.'

Unite Community branches have been growing. It now has more than 16,000 members campaigning around hospital closures and NHS cuts. In 2014, however, the local branches in Worksop, Chesterfield and Shirebrook set about a far more complex task: campaigning for full-time contracts for all staff at the Sports Direct warehouse with the goal of securing union recognition.

For Turner, this became a crucial campaign. 'Companies have always had some sort of core–periphery structure to the workforce,' Turner explains. 'You've got full-time staff with proper contracts protected against victimisation and arbitrary dismissal, possibly part of a union. That's the core. Then you've always had a periphery – this group of people around that are pooled in and out to deal with peaks and troughs. That used to be maybe 10/15 per cent of the workforce. Over the last five years you're seeing a complete switch – in some of our workplaces now you're finding 90 per cent of the workforce is agency. They're bought in on various contracts, under various mechanisms, through agencies or casual work and then find themselves pretty much permanently employed on-site. If you're not very careful, you find the union protecting and defending an ever-shrinking core of workers while the employers are constantly benchmarking the price of your labour versus the agency, or casual, or full self-employed.'

The union went after Sports Direct as the first target, in part because of owner Mike Ashley's brand. 'Ultimately, Sports

Direct have responsibility for their operation – and what they were doing was handing over £50 or £60 million a year to agencies and saying – you run the warehouse. And they ran it in the most appalling way – like a Dickensian workhouse.'

The company had already had some bad press about its working conditions. In 2013, when a former part-time sales assistant on a zero-hours contract sued the company, saying her employment rights had been breached, it was revealed that 90 per cent of the company's staff were on zero hours. Unite decided to take the company on across four different strands – investors, politicians, the media and the community. The idea, says Turner, was to manoeuvre the company into a corner where Unite became the best and only way out for them.

In early 2015 the union helped a team from Channel 4's *Dispatches* programme to go undercover at the warehouse. The resulting documentary branded Sports Direct a 'sweatshop' employing Victorian-era working conditions. Around the same time the union launched a confidential advice and support line for employees, as well as a national petition campaign in thirty cities that collected 20,000 signatures.

In September, the union briefed key shareholders ahead of the company's AGM, explaining their campaign and the company's business practices. They mounted a protest outside the meeting while Colin Hampton, who coordinated much of the direct action, read complaints about staff treatment to shareholders. A small-scale shareholder rebellion erupted, with just over half of shareholders voting against the directors' remuneration while 29 per cent, including the likes of Legal and General, supported a vote of no-confidence against chairman Keith Hellawell. Ashley's block shareholding ensured that neither attack succeeded, but he approached Hampton at the end of the meeting and promised to look into the forty-five-minute searches of employees after their working days were over.

In October 2015, the BBC's *Inside Out* team, tipped off by Unite, used an FOI request to discover that from January 2013 to December 2014, seventy-six ambulances or paramedic cars were sent to the warehouse. This included three calls about women experiencing pregnancy difficulties, including one who gave birth in the site's toilets. Unite then briefed friendly MPs, including Nottinghamshire's John Mann, who spoke to the *Daily Mail*, taking an 'English speakers can't get jobs' line.

In December 2015, the union helped two *Guardian* journalists get jobs at the factory, where they reported on hostile working conditions and how staff were fined for late clocking on, denied overtime for late clocking off and still made to wait, unpaid, for a security check at the end of a shift. Unite complained to HMRC that this meant staff were being paid less than the minimum wage. When the story broke, the Sports Direct share price started falling rapidly. The bad publicity started to affect trade – in January 2016, Sports Direct issued a profits warning after poor Christmas sales, while rival JD Sports said sales were up over 10 per cent during the same period. Parliament's business, innovation and skills committee announced it would investigate Sports Direct. As an investigation rumbled into life, Ashley announced a 15p-per-hour pay rise for staff currently taking less than the minimum wage.

With the outside pressure building, Unite returned to the community. In trying to raise Unite's profile around

Shirebrook, the first problem was fear. The agency workers were scared of their employers and scared of losing their jobs but also – with 95 per cent of the Sports Direct workers from Eastern Europe – they were very often fearful of unions as well. Having grown up understanding that trade unions had been arms of the communist state, they were wary of trading information with union reps.

Unite started working with the Polish churches. Priests happily opened up their church halls to meetings on weekend afternoons. They developed an English as a second language course, taught in churches, the Welfare Centre, out in Mansfield and as far as Worksop, reaching out to people by offering them help with the language as well as an official qualification. To help build this, they even supplied local shops with free bags, paid for by Unite. Every time someone visited a corner shop, they'd get a bag with a message from the union.

'We needed to build relationships with people we didn't have access to on-site,' says Luke Primarolo, the Unite organiser on the ground in Shirebrook. He's a deceptively young-looking forty-something and the man behind the English classes: 'We started thinking about this in October/November 2015, and recruited some volunteer teachers – a few retired heads of local schools, some from the congregations of local churches and some local folk who just wanted to get involved. In January 2016 we sat at a table outside the warehouse and tried to get people to sign up. At first we had nothing, but gradually more and more stopped by.'

The classes, Primarolo explains, weren't just about the language. They covered integrating, health and safety and how to organise. They also gave the union access to the workforce and to stories of life inside the warehouse. 'Soon we knew more about the company than it knew about itself,' he says with a slight smile.

With this fresh information, Unite briefed MPs and investors ahead of the committee hearing. The company dropped out of the FTSE100 in March 2016 after its share price fell over 40 per cent, wiping £2.3 billion from the retailer's value. In June, Unite, the agencies and Ashley himself gave evidence to the committee. Although far from contrite, Ashley admitted paying less than the minimum wage, agreed too many staff were on zero-hours contracts and claimed it wasn't his fault as he had little oversight over the company.

Protestors dressed as Dick Turpin, including, for the first time, agency workers, protested outside the Chesterfield office of Best Connection. In July 2016, Unite presented a resolution to leading fund managers, including Aberdeen Asset Management, Aviva, HSBC's investment arm, the Investor Forum and the Railways Pension Scheme at the TUC's headquarters in London. 'It's a new question for us – how do we build an alliance with shareholders who want to maximise their own return?' Turner explains. 'How do we get them to see the benefit of having a regulated work environment? We suggested to them that it isn't a sustainable business model – it's inherently conflicted and will remain so until the precarious nature of the work is addressed, and we would continue with our very public strategy to undermine the very nature of these businesses if necessary.'

In August, Sports Direct agreed to pay staff £1 million in missing pay after the HMRC concluded its investigation. The payments covered low pay as far back as May 2012. In September, it offered all its store staff full-time contracts.

Later that month, Sports Direct's largest institutional investors, including Standard Life, Aviva Investors, Legal and
General and Royal London, called on Mr Hellawell to step
down at the company's AGM, and issued demands for reform
of the board and corporate governance. He refused to go but
promised to step down the following September if a similar
vote was passed.

'We get internal pressures, asking if we can afford to keep
campaigning like this,' Turner confesses. 'But I say we can't
afford not to do it. Don't be under any illusions that your
employers are not looking at this business model. You are
right now being benchmarked against the cheapest possible
form of labour. And if they can do you in on Monday, they
will do you in on Monday. The only reason they don't is
because you've got power and influence.'

Back in Shirebrook, Primarolo is cautious. 'In the end,
this whole thing won't be a success until we can get these
people' – he gestures out at the dance floor, at the happy,
bobbing families and smooching couples – 'to have the
confidence to organise themselves. That's the next and most
difficult step.' He pauses, and gives a crooked smile.
'Although all the people here are agency workers – only two
of them weren't union members and tonight they signed up.
So anything's possible.'

Afterword

*A revolutionary moment in the world's history is a time for revolutions,
not patching.*

Sir William Beveridge, *Social Insurance
and Allied Services Report*

It's obvious that we have reached the end of the post-war era
of welfare – the proposals mapped out by Beveridge changed
the world, saved lives, educated children, boosted productivity and, by removing the worst effects of poverty, helped
the country heal after the horrors of war. The children of the
report remade British culture – allowing talent to flourish
regardless of background. Those proposals were as revolutionary as he hoped – but the world has changed and is
changing still.

The Five Giants are returning, and the need for a comprehensive response is as urgent, but we can't go back and reuse
Beveridge's solutions. He produced detailed and specific
proposals for a particular time. We have to find a new

consensus based on his first principle – that the purpose of a government is the happiness of its people.

We are at a potentially revolutionary moment – the chance to remake society is tangible. The alternative – the slow sink back into the desperation of the 1930s or even the barbarism of the Victorian era – is equally possible.

On the one hand this requires strong institutions and bold leadership. The post-war Keynesian state is gone. The private sector has had its chance to build a richer, fairer, happier society and it has failed. So this leadership must come from the bottom up – from the people who deal with weighty problems day after day, creating imaginative, simple solutions. The answers to many of our problems are already out there, already being practised, already succeeding. We need to open the lines of communication, reclaim the social. We need – urgently – collaboration, innovation and community building.

But we also need – and deserve – more. When Seebohm Rowntree measured poverty in York for the first time, from 1899 to 1901, one in five children died before they reached their first birthday – 40 per cent were dead by the time they reached fourteen. By the time he conducted his second survey in 1936, child mortality rates had improved dramatically – 80 per cent of children celebrated their fifteenth birthday. In 1941, Rowntree published *Poverty and Progress*, recognising that progress had been made, arguing there was more to be done and declaring optimistically that this could be achieved. His ideas shaped Beveridge's thinking; he worked on the Beveridge Report and helped to pioneer family allowances. When he published his third survey in 1950, the *Times* wrote that there had been 'a remarkable improvement – no less than the virtual abolition of the sheerest want'. Like Rowntree in 1936, we can't be satisfied with protecting what we have achieved – we must frame our next steps and aim for more and better.

George Orwell was also surveying poverty in 1936 – he wrote *The Road to Wigan Pier* before heading off to fight in the Spanish Civil War. By 1941 – as Rowntree was publishing and Beveridge starting work – he published *The Lion and the Unicorn*, a vision of a British revolution. He talked about England – but the sentiment applies today to all of us. He wrote,

> England has got to be true to herself. She is not being true to herself while the refugees who have sought our shores are penned up in concentration camps, and company directors work out subtle schemes to dodge their Excess Profits Tax. The heirs of Nelson and of Cromwell are not in the House of Lords. They are in the fields and the streets, in the factories and the armed forces, in the four-ale bar and the suburban back garden; and at present they are still kept under by a generation of ghosts. Compared with the task of bringing the real England to the surface, even the winning of the war, necessary though it is, is secondary. By revolution we become more ourselves, not less. There is no question of stopping short, striking a compromise, salvaging 'democracy', standing still. Nothing ever stands still. We must add to our heritage or lose it, we must grow greater or grow less, we must go forward or backward. I believe in England, and I believe that we shall go forward.

Index

Page numbers in **bold** refer to figures, page numbers in *italic* refer to tables

Aalborg University, Centre for
    Comparative Welfare Studies 28
Abrahams, Debbie 73
absolute poverty 21–2
Action Homeless 130, 131
Adams, Jonathan 119–20
Adamson, Mike 76
Adlington, David 204
Advisory Group on Contraception 188
Africa 21, 36, 68–9
Age UK 42
Agency Worker Regulations 106
agency workers 227
    education 227–8
    numbers 86
    rights 106–7
    umbrella companies 106–12
    see also employment agencies;
    temporary workers
Alby (employment agency client) 84–5
Alexander, Shona 192
Alice (Star Project's service user) 62
Amazon 55, 85, 88
ambulances 76

Amec 177
AMECO 36
Arcadia group 94
area-based premiums 30
Argos 93
Armstrong, Andrew 215
Arthur, Daniel 16–7
Ashley, Mike 86–7, 224, 225–6, 226, 228
ASOS 88
Association of North East Councils 147, 173
Association of Retained Council
    Housing 124
Atlanco 196
Atlantic Philanthropies 218–20
Atos 72
Attlee, Clement 3
austerity 147, 173, 183–4
average earnings, real value 18
Aziz (homeless man) 20–1, 29

baby booms 39, 47–8
baby boomers 40
Bailey, Jeremy 155–6
Bailey, Nick 125

bank accounts 30, 89, 92
basic needs 10–1
BBC 76, 163, 187, 197, 226
Beaseley, Paul 88
Beatrice Webb Society 29
Beckham, David 48
Belfast 176–7, 216, 218
Bellamy, Richard 8, 207–8
benefit cap 53–4
benefit claimants, demonisation 11
benefit fraud 11–3
benefit sanctions 135, 143, 145–7, 148–9,
    150, 177–8, 207
Benefits (TV series) 49
Benefits Street (TV series) 116
Bentley 99
Best Connection 86–7, 226
Beth (child poverty victim) 113–4
Bevan, Anthony 205
Bevan Healthcare 77–8
Beveridge, William, and the Beveridge
    Report 1–4, 9–10, 12, 15, 21, 25,
    37, 38–9, 47–8, 74, 115, 124, 179,
    191–2, 230–1
Bibby, John 121, 212–3
Biggs, Lewis 208
bills, arrears 17
Billy (Folkestone gold digger) 209–11
black health economy 64, 149
Blackpool 74
Blair, Tony 22
Blue Arrow 96–9
Bolsover Council 91
Brexit 4, 165, 167, 170, 201
Briggs, Ben 105
Briggs, Joanne 104
BrightHouse 33–4, 35
Brighton 146
British Cohort Study, 1970 57
British Dental Health Foundation 64
British Election Study 170
British Household Panel Survey 117
British National Party 167
British Social Attitudes 49
broadband 24, 137–9, **137**, 169
Burslem 169
Buttery, Father Graeme 172, 174, 180
Buy-As-You-View 33, 34

Caerphilly 160
Caerphilly Observer 160
Callum (youth centre volunteer) 147–50
Campaign for Contraception 188–9
Caplovitz, David 29–30
Cardiff 10, 120, 144, 152, 154, 164, 197, 199
Care Quality Commission 42–3
care workers 46–7
Carlyle, Thomas 198
Carney, Mark 19
Carr, Jimmy 12
cash work 148–9
Castle Point, Essex 5
casualisation, and impoverishment
    96–106
Cawley, Ian 175–9
Central and North West London
    (CNWL) NHS Foundation Trust
    186–8
Centre for Comparative Welfare Studies,
    Aalborg University 28
Centre for Research on Socio-Cultural
    Change 43
Centre for Social Justice 139
Centre for Workforce Intelligence 71–80
Chalmers, Lisa 35
Channel 4 116, 225
Channel Tunnel 206–7
Charlesworth, J. J. 209
Chartered Institute of Housing 54
child benefit 11, 48, 49, 50
child mortality rates 74, 231
child poverty 14, 22, 169, 173, 231
    definition 26–7
    Hartlepool 177
    health implications 54
    and parental behaviour 27–8
    transience and 113–5
Child Poverty Act 21
child tax credit 48, 50–5, 111
children 6, 69–70, 74–5
children's allowances 48
Children's Society 33, 53, 114
China 104, 172
Chinese cockle pickers 87
Church Action on Poverty 78
Cincinnati Post 157–8
Citizens Advice Bureau 33, 34, 71, 136,
    142, 192, 202

Clark, Alan 172, 174–5
Coal Industry Social Welfare
    Organisation 192
coalition government 22, 26, 72, 119, 123
Coates, Karen 64
Combined Homelessness and
    Information Network 126
community service 136
computers 24, 34, 35
    access 133–7, 142
Conservative governments 25, 116, 117–8
corporation tax 35
Corus 155
cost of living 23
Cottingham 94
council housing 115–6
councils
    corruption scandals 159–60
    funding cuts 183–4
County Fermanagh 214–22
courier services 101–2
credit 31–5
crime 177
Crisis 10, 126
Crook, Peter 33
Curtis, Adrian 78–9
Cyprus 221

Daily Mirror 197
Dalglish, Kenny 12
Dan (ex-soldier) 213–4
De Haan, Roger 206, 208
Dearne Valley 171
debt 23, 32, 33
deindustrialisation 64–5
delivery services 16–7, 101–2
Denmark 28
DentAid 66–9, 76
DenTek 63
dentistry, DIY
    experience of 60–3, 67–8
    extent 63–4, 66
dentists, charges 60, 62, 63, 68–9
Department for Communities and Local
    Government 120, 121
Department of Education 54
Department of Health 78
Department of Work and Pensions 12,
    26–7, 49, 73, 146

deprivation 169, 183–4
    and GP coverage 70–1
    Hartlepool 172–9
    measures of poverty 23–6
destitution 6–9
developing countries, poverty rates 15
Dewsbury 66–9
DHL 95, 96–7
Digital by Default programme 139
digital democracy deficit 138–9
digital deprivation 133–45
    broadband 137–9, **137**
    computer access 133–7, 142
    Universal Credit 139–45
digital inclusion strategy 137
disability-free life 72, 74
Dispatches 225
disposable income 14–5, 26
Doctors of the World 76
domestic violence 184
doorstep lenders 32–3
drugs and drug abuse 127, 177
Duncan, David 73
Duncan Smith, Iain 22–3, 26, 53–4, 139
Dundee 79
Dunfermline 88
Durham, County 117

East, Nick 133, 144–5
East Midlands Ambulance 91–2
Eastern Europeans 82–3, 84, 88–9
EatFirst 101
Economic and Social Research Council
    13–4, 17, 146–7
economic growth 3, 31–2
EDL (English Defence League) 171
education, shared 215–22
Egan, Owen 215
elderly
    care budget 41–2
    experience of 39–40, 41
    over-sixty-fives 39, 42
    in poverty 40–1
    quality of care 46–7
    supporting 54
election campaign, 2015 11
Elizabeth Stories 48
Ellis, Stephen 151
Emily 125–6

employment, full 3
employment agencies 81–95
  activities 85
  agency worker numbers 86
  charges 92
  deductions 92
  disciplinary process 89–90
  Eastern Europeans 82–3, 88–90
  employment practices 87–95
  health and safety 91–2
  history and development 85
  lack of British-born persons 82
  licensing regime 85
  mandatory sign up 86
  people as commodities 82–3
  people trafficking 89
  profits 81
  recruitment 88–9
  regulation 87–8
  salary sacrifice scheme 87–8
  sign ups 82
  strike system 91
  wages 83
  working in 81–5
Employment and Support Allowance 73, 124, 131–2
English Housing Survey 115
Enniskillen 214–5, 216–7, 219–21
Equity Release Council. 40
equity release lending 40
Erika (care worker) 46–7
essential needs 23–6
Essex, Castle Point 5
EU referendum 4, 165, 200
  voter motivation 167–8, 169–70, 170–5
  voter turnout 167
  voting patterns 4–5, 170
EURES (European Employment Services) 88–90
European Commission, Directorate General for Economic and Financial Affairs 36
European Union 4, 5

Facundo (Spanish worker) 101–3
Fairbridge 107–12
fairness 29
Family Expenditure Survey 58
Family Resources Survey 58

family size 47–55
Farmers Guardian 105
farmers and farming 51–3, 103–6, 106
Feeney, Chuck 218
Fermanagh Community Trust 215–22, 217–8, 222
Financial Conduct Authority 33
Financial Partnership LLP 109
Financial Service Authority 34
financialisation 42
Finlay, Dermot 220
Five Giant Evils, the 3–4, 231–2
Flynn, Daniel 169–70
Folkestone 6–9, 203–11, 212
food banks 78–80, 181–2, 207
food costs 30–1, *31*
for-profit care homes 42, 43–5
Foster, Ben 215
Four Seasons 43–4, 45
FrameWorks Institute 10–1
free market economics 15
fuel tariffs 30
Full Fact 11

Gangmasters Licensing Authority 87–8
Gardiner, Hazel 220
General Dynamics 200
Generation X 58
gig economy 86
Gingerbread 181–2
Gladwell. Malcolm 164
Glamorgan Gates 195–6, 199–200
Glasgow 60, 65, 117, 125, 144
globalisation 15
Gloucestershire County Council 106
GMB 18, 120
Goodwin, Matthew 5, 170
Gowland, Peter 172, 175
GPs 62, 63, 64, 70–1, 144, 193
Gray, Jane 126–7, 193
Green, Philip 12
Gregg, Paul 117
gross domestic product 3
Guardian 90–3, 226
Gurner, Richard 160

Hague, William 196
Hammond, Jim 55, 56
Hammond, Tony 56–7

Hampton, Colin 225
Hands, Guy 43
hardship payments 146, 150
Harris, Mike 138–9
Hartlepool 147–50, 172–80
Hartlepool Hospital 174
Headway 131
Health and Social Care Act, 2012 186
health inequality 71–80
　access to care 144
　black market health economy 149
　cost 75
　cost analysis 73–4
　crisis 76–80
　economic advantages of equal
　　opportunities 75
　GP coverage 70–1
　oral 60–9
　and poverty 29
　waiting times 76
Heart Community Centre, Hartlepool
　175, 177–9
heart disease 73
Heath, Oliver 5, 170
Heidi (housing officer) 130
Hermes 101
Heseltine, Michael 117–8
Hiley, Anna 126–7, 193
Hinds, Damian 142
Hodgson, Lesley 193–202
Hodgson, Roy 12
holding farms 89
Homebase 93
homeless hostels 20–1
homelessness 99
　Eastern Europeans 84
　experience of 7, 127–32
　healthcare 126–7, 131–2
　increase in 121–2
　rough sleepers 126–32
　system bureaucracy 131
　total numbers 126
hospitals 45–6, 62–3, 76, 174
household debt 32
household goods 25
household income 5, 14, 21, 58
HouseMark 124–5
housing
　affordable 212–3

building 115
council 115–6
demolitions 119–20
empty 120
hazards 115
managed decline 117–20
private rental sector 113–5, 120–1,
　123–4
rent arrears 125
rent statistics, VOA 123
right-to-buy 116, 120
shortage 118–9, 120
standards 114–5
transience 113–5
housing benefit 7, 12, 99, 107, 110, 112,
　116, 122–5, 140, 194
Housing Market Renewal Pathfinder
　Programme 118, 119–20
Howe, Geoff 118
Howells, Rachel 152–3, 154, 158–9,
　160–5
HS1 high-speed rail link 208–9
Hughes, Anwen 51–3
Hughes, Joanne 218–9, 221
hunger 78–80
Hunt, Tristram 166
Hutin, Mike 154–5
Hythe, Alex and Tilly 60–3

I, Daniel Blake (film) 13, 72–3
Imani (single parent) 181–2
immigration 167, 171, 175, 193, 196–202
impoverishment, and casualisation
　96–106
inclusion 126–7
Inclusion Healthcare 84, 193
income 58–9
　disposable 14–5, 26
　growth 26
　margins 17
　women 182–3
Independent 86–7
Index of Multiple Deprivation 147, 172
industry, competitiveness 3
inequality 3, 14, 26, 35
　oral health 65–9
infant mortality 75
inflation 21, 37
Inside Housing blog 119

Inside Out 226
Institute for Fiscal Studies 14
Institute for Public Policy Research 122
Institute of Fiscal Studies 58
insurance 30
interest rates 32–4
internet access 24, 169
IRA 214, 216

Jack (bricklayer) 140–1
James, Alice 167
James Cook Hospital 174
Jenkins, Paul 79–80
job creation 15
job security 37
Jobcentres 24, 86, 112, 133–5, 142, 145, 178
    sanctions 145–7, 148–9, 150
Jobseeker's Allowance 12, 21, 73, 134,
    135, 139–40
Johnson, Oliver 139
Johnston Press 152
Jordan (temporary worker) 96–101
Joseph, Keith 118
Joseph Rowntree Foundation 4–6, 5–6,
    10, 14, 18, 24–5, 36, 40, 116–7, 170,
    183–4
Joseph Rowntree Housing Trust 4
Journal of Dental Research 69

Kavanagh, Dr Jayne 184–9
Kelly Louise (temporary accommodation
    resident) 122
Kennan, Gerry 55
Kentucky Fried Chicken. 93
Kilpatrick, Dean 204, 206
Kings Fund 75–6
Knott, John 205–6

Labour Force Survey 42, 58, 58–9, 86,
    94, 117
labour market, flexible 15
Labour Party 3, 117, 167, 170–1
LaingBuisson 45
Lancashire County Council 41–2
language, of poverty 29
Lansley, Stewart 23–4
Larsen, Christian Albrekt 28
Laughlin McCann, Ruairi 108
Lazarsfeld, Paul 164

Leicester 81–5, 126–32, 193
Leona 144
Lewis, Kenneth 85
libraries 134, 135, 136, 142, 144–5, 211
life expectancy 72, 205
Liverpool, Speke 136–7, 143
living standards 24, 26
Local Data Company 65
Local Government Association 45
local government, funding gap 45
Local Housing Allowance 122–4
local newspapers, closures 151–65
Local World 152, 156
London 21, 118, 120, 125–6
lone parents 79
Longden, John 145–6
low pay 35–6
low-income families 27, 30, 54, 65, 120, 138
Lucas, Patricia 69
Lyon Bowley, Arthur 21

McCabe, Angus 189–90
McCusker, Lauri 215–22
McDermott, Sean 215
McDonalds 93, 99
Macedonia 215, 221
Mack, Joanna 13–4, 23–4
McKenzie, Lisa 189
Macmillan Lindsey 117
Major, John 72
malnutrition 78–80
Manchester 10, 20–1, 30, 39, 56, 72, 118,
    123
Mann, John 226
ManpowerGroup 81–5
manufacturing industry, collapse in 59
Margaret Pyke Centre 184–9
Mark (*Big Issue* vendor) 76–8
Mark (short-hours contract worker) 93–4
Markowski, Erwin 89
Markowski, Krystian 89
Marmot, Sir Michael 71–5
Marmot Review 71–5
Mason, Paul 31–2
Maude, Francis 137
MAXIMUS 72
Maxwell, Dr 131–2
May, Emily 107–12
means testing 25–6

Measuring Child Poverty 22
media coverage 12, 13, 28, 151–65
Merthyr Tydfil 193–202
middle class 17
Middlesbrough 74, 117, 172–9
migrant workers 193, 196–202
Milford Haven 159–60
millennials 58–9
Milroy, Hugh 213–4
Milroy, Vicky 103–6
miners strike, 1984–5 223
Miners' Welfare Institutes 192
Minimum Income Standard 24–5
minimum wage 83, 86, 92, 94, 99, 181, 226, 228
Mistry, Robert 47
mobile phones, pre-pay 143–4
Money Advice Service 33
Moore, Martin 156, 157
Moorin, Michelle 205
moral responsibility 4
Morecambe Bay 87
Morrissey, Helena 48
Morse, Andrew 192
MPs 152
Mullins, Len 159–60

National Association of Citizens Advice Bureau 71
National Audit Office 13, 146
National Centre for Social Research 10
National Child Development Study 117
National Council for Voluntary Organisations 190
National Farmers Union 104–5
National Federation of Arm's Length Management Organisations 124
National Health Insurance 62
National Institute for Health and Care Excellence 46
National Insurance 12, 16, 74, 88, 93, 106–8, 110
national living wage 14, 26
neoliberalism 15, 212
Nettleton, Barbara 190–1
Network Rail 99
New Enterprise Allowance scheme 107, 110–1
New Labour 25–6, 118

New Look 99
new poor, the 14
New Zealand 36
Newcastle 118, 133–6, 142, 192, 199
Newcastle Airport 17
Newcastle University 64
newspapers, local 151–65
Newsquest 152, 160
Newtownbutler 220–1
NHS
    budget cuts 76
    GPs 62, 63, 64, 70–1, 144, 193
    dental services 65–6
    draft sustainability and transformation plans 76
    finances 75–6
Nisa 96–7
Noakes, Terry 209
Northern Ireland 63, 76, 176, 214–22
Norway 105
Nuttall, Paul 167

obesity 73
O'Donovan, Nick 66–7
O'Dowd, John 221
Ofcom 137–8, 144
Office for Budget Responsibility 37
Office for National Statistics 14–5, 32, 49, 50, 78
Oliver, Jamie 48
Open Hands 132
oral health inequality 65–9, 69
Orchid Consultancy Ltd 108, 110
Orwell, George
    The Lion and the Unicorn 231
    Road to Wigan Pier 55, 136, 190, 231
Orwell Prize 18
Osborne, George 53, 72, 141
O'Sullivan, Anthony 160
out-of-work families 49
Outtrim, Roger 39–40, 41, 59
Oxfam 78, 140
Oxford Economics 120

Paisley, Renfrewshire 60–3, 64–5
parental behaviour 27–8
Parfitt, Rick 12
Parry-Jones, Bryn 160
part-time work, increase in 86

Patel, Dipen Hasmukhbai 108–9
Patha, Pramod 108
payday loan companies 33
Pembrokeshire Herald 159–60
pension credits 12
pensioners 40
pensions 38–9, 50
people trafficking 89
PerfectHome 33, 34
Phipps, Andy 95
Pioneer Business Consulting 108
Poland 89
police and policing 174, 191
Porchlight 210, 211
Port Talbot 152–7, 158–9, 160–4
Port Talbot Guardian 152, 153, 154–5,
        156, 158–9
Port Talbot Magnet 160–4
poverty 173, 181–2, 231–2
    absolute 21–2
    benchmark 22–3
    culture of 116
    definition 5–6, 20–6
    Denmark 28
    deprivation measures of 23–6
    developing countries 15
    escape chances 54
    and family size 48–9
    health implications 29, 54
    images 36
    language of 29
    media coverage 28
    official figures 14
    pensioners in 40–1
    public attitudes to 10–1
    relative income 21, 22–3
    responsibility for 26–8
    rise in 13–4, 35
    suburbanisation of 125
    Sweden 28–9
    systemic 13, 27–37, *31*
    working households 36–7
Poverty and Social Exclusion project,
        Economic and Social Research
        Council 13–4, 17
poverty premium 29–35, *31*
poverty threshold 21–2
precarious pay penalty 94–5
pregnancy difficulties 92, 226

prescription charges 63, 71
Press Association 165
press gazette 152
Primarolo, Luke 227–8, 229
private care home sector, collapse of
        42–3
Private Eye 35
productivity gap 4
Proudlove, Dave 118
Provident Financial 32–3
public attitudes 10–1
public spending, coalition governement
        cuts 26
Purdam, Kingsley 30–1, *31*

Qualitycourse Ltd 87–8
Queen's University, Belfast 218
Quirk, Padraic 218, 219, 221

Rachman, Becky 206
racism 201
Rainbow Centre, Folkestone 8, 9
Randstad 85
RCB 100
Real Junk Food Project 66–7
Real Junk Tooth Project 66–9
Rebecca (Universal Credit claimant) 143
recession, 2008 33, 60, 140, 172
Red Cross 76
Redcar Steelworks 172–3
regeneration 208
relative income poverty 21, 22–3
rent arrears 121, 124, 125
rent-to-own companies 33–5
residential care
    collapse of 42–3
    costs 41
    for-profit care homes 42, 43–4
    funding 44–5
    lack of places 45–6
Resolution Foundation 10, 58–9, 86, 94,
        107
respect, lack of 171
retail sector 59, 169
Richardson, Emma 60, 71
right-to-buy 116, 120
riots, 1981 117–8
Rob (farm manager) 103
Rooney, Wayne 12

rough sleepers 126–32
Rowntree, Seebohm 3, 4, 21, 23–4, 231–2
Royal British Legion 6, 7
Royal College of General Practitioners 70
Royston, Sam 27, 53

Saga 41, 206
St Merryn 196–8, 202
Save the Children 30, 32–3
Savills 105–6
Schulhofer-Wohl, Sam 158
Scott (temporary worker) 96–101
Scottish independence referendum 170, 171
self-employed workers 102–3, 107–12
self-medicating 68
settlements, classification 117
Sevacare 47
Shah, Jayesh Javerchand 109
Shared Education Act 215
Sheena (cleaner) 70–1
Sheffield 16, 144
Shelter 10, 114–5, 121, 122, 123, 126, 212–3
shipbuilding 173, 175–6
Shirebrook 86–7, 88–93, 95, 222–9
short-hours contracts 93–4
sickness benefit 211
Siemiatkowski, Sebastian 28
Singh, Jas 127–32
single parents 181–2
Skipper, Clare 67–8
Smith, Sid 55
Smith, Trevor 55–6
social cleansing 116
social insurance 140
Social Insurance and Allied Services Report see Beveridge, William
social justice 13
social mobility 56–8, 175, 179
social reform 2
solutions 212–29, 230–1
Sopp, Graham and Lisa 6–9
South Wales Evening Post 155–6, 159
Spain 31, 101, 102
Speke, Liverpool 136–7, 143
Sports Direct 86–7, 88–93, 222–9
squatting 128
Staffline 196–7

standard of living 24, 26
Star Project 62
stereotypes 80
Stockton 174
Stoke-on-Trent 97–101, 118, 119, 166–70
strike system 91
subsistence 21, 25
Sunday Mirror 93–4
Sunderland 184
Sunshine House, Wigan 135–6, 190–1
supermarket price wars 105
Surrey Dock Solutions 108, 110
Sutton-in-Ashfield 189
Sweden, attitude to benefits 28–9
Switzerland 36
systemic poverty 13, 27–37, *31*

Tannock, Stuart 197–8
Tata Steel 155, 161, 162–3, 172–3
tax and tax revenues 3, 12, 35, 103, 110
tax avoidance 12, 13
tax havens 35
taxpaying population 54
Taylor, Jon 88
Taylor, Matthew 103
Teaching Talent 107–8
telephones 24
temporary accommodation 122
temporary workers 85
    deductions 99
    promises made to 98, 99
    shifts 98
    working conditions 96–101
    see also agency workers; employment agencies
Terra Firma 43–4
Tesco 93–4, 105, 109
Thatcher, Margaret 72
336 contracts 89
Time Exchange, Hartlepool 178–9
Toumba, Jack 65
Toynbee Hall, Whitechapel 2
Trades Union Congress 15, 102–3
transience 113–5
Transitional Care Education Services Ltd (TCES) 107, 109–10
Transline 86–9, 91
Transline Polska 88–9
travel costs 31, 100, 182

Trinity Mirror 152, 156–7
Troubled Families 22
Trussell Trust 78–80
Turner, Paul 73
Turner, Stephen 223–5, 229
2 Sisters Food Group 202

umbrella companies 106–12
uncertainty 19
unemployment 3, 10, 142, 173, 205
unemployment benefit 25–6, 50, 140
unemployment system 145–7
Unicef 221
Unison 46, 47
Unite 92, 223–9
Unite Community 223–4
United Kingdom Independence Party
        166–7, 171, 193, 200–1
universal benefits 25–6
Universal Credit 24, 26, 50, 107, 124–5,
        136, 139, 139–42, 143, 178
Universal Jobmatch 133–5, 150
University of Bristol 30
University of Glamorgan 195–6
University of Manchester 30–1, *31*
Unreported Britain project 18
Upton, Matthew 34

Valuation Office Agency 123
vandalism 147
Veteran's Aid 212
    welfare to well-being programme
        213–4
Veterans Council 191
Vision House, Suite F1–F3 108–9

wages 16–7
    employment agencies 83
    falling 5, 36
    median pay 53–4
    precarious pay penalty 94–5
    real value 18
    short-hours contracts 94
    zero hours contracts 94–5
Wales 119–20, 192, 193–202
Walker, Malcolm 172–3
warehouse working conditions 90–3, 95,
        96–9
Webb, Sydney and Beatrice 2

Weir, Peter 221
Welby, Justin, Archbishop of Canterbury
        9
welfare, public attitudes to 10
welfare budget 50
welfare cuts, coalition governement 26
welfare state 2, 3
welfare to well-being programme,
        Veteran's Aid 213–4
welfare-to-work New Deal 25
Wellings, Richard 208–9
Welsh Assembly 153–4
Wenger, Arsène 12
Western Mail 156–7
Wigan 55–7, 135–6, 190–1
Wildman, John 64
Wiles, Colin 119
Wilson, Bob 136–7
Wilson, Ian 68
winter fuel allowance 50
Wokingham 74
women
    activism 189–93
    ethnic minority 183
    incomes 182–3
    pregnancy difficulties 92
    protests 189
    rough sleepers 127
    sexual health and contraception
        184–9
    single parents 181–2
    status 191–2
    visibility 189
    wage gap 183
Women's Aid 10, 184
Women's Budget Group 182–3
women's refuges 184
Wonga 33
Work Capability Assessment 72–4
Working Tax Credit 50–1, 141, 143
workless families, myth of 116–7
World Bank 15
Wright, Lisa 135–6

YouGov 17
Young, Andrew 142

zero-hours contracts 16, 86, 89, 93, 94–5,
        222–9